Investing for Beginners:

2 Manuscript: Options Trading Beginners Guide, Options Trading Advanced Guide

By

Mark Elder, Brian Douglas

Options Trading:

Beginner's Guide to Make Money with Options Trading – All the Strategies to Create an Important Income, in a Short Time

Options Trading:

Advanced Guide to Make Money Trading Options in 30 Days or Less! – Learn the Fundamentals and Profitable Strategies of Options Trading

Options Trading:

Beginner's Guide to Make Money with Options Trading – All the Strategies to Create an Important Income, in a Short Time

By

Mark Elder, Brian Douglas

6

Introduction

Trading the market comes with so many options that you can use; it all depends on your choice and preferences. When you choose certain security, you need to know that it is different from other securities. This book focuses on Options trading and goes ahead to define what it is so that you know what makes it different from other securities on the market.

Options trading is one of the most popular securities that you can trade. This book covers the various concepts of trading as well as what to do to succeed as a new trader. Seasoned traders also have a chance to add to their knowledge when they find aspects of the book that they didn't know before.

The book explores the basics of trading; giving you concepts that get you started. This is a part of a series, meaning you can go for other titles in the book to give you an advanced look at options trading.

Mistakes happen, and when they do, you need to find a solution to these problems. The book explores the different mistakes that happen in trading and look at the solutions that you can explore.

Who is This Book For?

The book is aimed at both novices and seasoned traders alike. Novices can use the book as a stepping stone to advanced techniques, while seasoned traders can use the book as a reference to understand the basics.

Chapter 1: Options Trading Basics

Options trading refers to a contractual agreement between two parties in which the buying party gets the right to trade a security at a predetermined price and at a predetermined date. The right, however, is not obligatory in nature. The right is given to the buyer by the seller through the payment of premiums. Options trading involves trading with stocks and securities for the purpose of profit and also keen to avoid incurring losses. In options trading, the buyer is also referred to as the taker in the contract. The seller is usually referred to as the writer.

Types of Options Trading

There are two types of options trading that grant two different rights. The first one is termed as call options. They give the buyer rights to purchase the asset that is underlying the contract on a later date depending at a predetermined price. This right is, however, not obligatory and is usually based on the discretion of the taker or the contract and his understanding of the market performance in the course of the life of the contract. The life of the contract refers to the period before the contract expires. The price of buying the contract is termed as the exercise price. Sometimes it is also referred to as the strike price.

An example of call options is if Santos Limited has a contract available with shares on security that has the last sale price of $6.00. If the contract has a three-month expiry period, the taker then has the option of offering the shares for a call of $6.00. One can buy 100 token offerings of securities at the said call price per share at the time of choice for the taker in the course of the life of the contract. The taker is also required to pay premiums to the writer of the contract for the option. To fully own the call rights, one has to exercise it based on the predetermined dates that are specified in the agreement.

On the hand, the writer of the contract has an obligation to ensure that the shares that are purchased are delivered. In the above example, the writer has to deliver 100 security token offerings as long as the taker of the contract has exercised the option. However, the writer sustains reception of option premium during the life of the contract regardless of Put whether or not the taker exercises the option.

The other form of options is the put options. These ones are designed to grant the taker rights of selling the underlying assets for a price that has been predetermined by the contract. The rights to sell have to be exercised in the course of the life of the contract. Just like the call options, the taker of the contract is not compelled to exercise the right. In this case, the buyer only provides the shares required in the agreement if the put right is exercised.

An example of a put option is when a contract by the writer has a predetermined $6.00 put token offering for a predetermined period of three months. The taker has a put option of selling 100 security token offerings as shares at the said price of $6.00 per share. This sell right has to be exercised in eth active life of the contract by the date of expiry of the agreement.

As with the call option, the taker still has to pay premiums to the writer for the contract and the trade to be valid. The right is only valid when it is exercised with the course of the life of the contract. Outside of it, the right is forfeited regardless of whether or not value was created out of the contract. This means that the taker of the contract has to be keen on market performance and judge well whether or not to invoke the sell rights and when. Sometimes, a taker will opt not to exercise the right of sale of shares as the contract expiry dies out.

The exercise style is usually dependent on the system used. Two systems are usually used: the American style and the European style. The European style usually compels the taker to exercise the right in the contract only on the expiry date. The American style is more flexible and allows the exercise of the right any time before the date of expiry of the agreement.

Advantages of Option Trading

Option trading has many advantages for investors. Essentially, it is an investment that offers an opportunity for those who have the capital to delve into an income generation venture. Advantages with options trading are multiple and should motivate people into the sector of trading securities, selling and buying assets as well as earning interests that accrue.

First is the ability of this venture to aid to manage risks when investing in stocks and securities. They can cushion one from having to incur losses in investment. This is because investing in the stocks and shares usually involves risks of all in the value of the shares. This devaluation can lead to a dwindling of the profits and may, in fact, cut into the shares that one holds. However, the options marketing ensure that one is hedged from such uncertainty and as well as guarantees that a person can earn value from the trading of the shares.

Options trading is also advantageous is it allows someone the time to decide about purchase or not. This is particularly the advantage of the call options. The contract usually has a period during which a person considers the exercise of the implied rights. The person studies the market and its performance and has the allowance to understand his financial situation before making a decision on whether to purchase the shares or not. This leads one to make decisions about investments that are reasoned out. It always comes with more preparedness to handle the consequences of the decisions that one takes. This helps to rid the habit of making trading decisions on whims that can later lead to anxiety and worry as market forces swing into play.

The freedom of action to exercise an option is also an exciting aspect of trading. This is because this is a speculative filed based on eth analysis of market forces and performance. Once one enters an option contract, they can happily enjoy trading them without the obligation to exercise the rights included in the contract. One can, in fact, just understand the market landscape and opt for a trade investment with an option that one does not even have intentions of exercising. On the speculative conception of options trading, one can decide to just exercise the purchase right in a call option when they know the market environment is getting better and promises value. They can also decide to exercise the sell option when losses are expected to avoid the loss or salvage a profit margin.

Leverage

Leverage is a very advantageous aspect of options trading that people try to take advantage of and participate in the security market. In leverage, one has to place smaller outlays with a prospect of making higher profits in view. This encourages those who do not have the capital to invest in the underlying assets or shares to find a way of investing and get returns. One of the important parts of leverage is that one is usually getting back returns from the underlying assets or shares, yet they have not been required to pay the full cost for the purchase of the shares.

In the idea of leverage also is also the advantage of diversification. This by creating a portfolio without incurring huge initial outlays. This diversification can then create a stream of investment channels that in practice, lead to profits increasing one's earnings. Sometimes this income can increase to go above one's dividends when one takes call options that are laid again the shares owned. This extra income can even emanate from the shares that are integrated having been acquired from a lending facility. Option premiums also come ahead of the trading activities and hence cushioning one from any chances of loss.

Components of an Option Contract

There are various standardized components of option contracting that enable ease in engaging in options trading. These components characterize the mechanics of how options trading binds the parties involved and demonstrates the ay profits can be generated if the market forces are favorable. Among the components of options trading are:

- Underlying securities

- Contract size

- Expiry day

- Exercise prices

Underlying securities

Options that are traded on the market only apply to certain assets. These assets are then referred to as underlying securities. The word shares can be replaced with the word shares in certain instances. There are companies that provide the asset against which the option operators list options. ASX is one operator in the options trading market has played a key role in the listing of underlying securities.

The term classes of options refer to the listing of puts and calls as options of the same assets. As an example, is when puts and calls are applied to a lease corporation's shares. This does not put in regard the contract terms in terms of the predetermined price or duration of expiry of the call and put contracts. An operator of options trading usually provides the list of the available classes for the benefit of investors.

Contract Size

On the ASX platform of options trading, the market standardizes the size of the option contract at 100 underlying securities. One option contract, therefore, corresponds to 100 underlying shares. The changes that can happen only come when reorganization happens on the initial outlay of the underlying share or the capital therein. Index options usually fix the value of the contract at a certain stipulated dollar rate.

Expiry day

Options are constrained by time and have a life span. There are predetermined expiry deadlines that the platform operator sets which have to be respected. These deadlines are usually rigid, and once they are out the rights under a contract in a particular class of unexercised options are then forfeited. Usually, the last day of the life span of a contract is the summative trading date. For shares that have their expiry coming by June of 2020, the options over them have their last trading day on a Thursday that comes before the last Friday that happens to be in the month. Those that expire beyond June 2020, expiry is on the third Thursday that happens to be in the month. For index options.

Expiries come on the concurrent third Thursday of the same month of writing the option. However, these dates can be readjusted by the options platform operator as and when there is a reason for such action.

In recent years, platform operators have introduced more short-term options for some underlying. Some are weekly, while others are on a fortnightly basis. These ones have the corresponding weekly or fortnightly expiries. When the life span of options run out, the operators then create new deadlines. However, all classes of options have their expiries subject to quarters of the financial calendar.

Exercise Prices

These are the buying price or the price of selling the assets or underlying securities. These prices are also called strike prices. They are usually predetermined in the option contract and have to be met if one has to exercise the rights in an option. Essentially, they are called exercise because the parties are now invoking the rights that are stipulated in an option either to buy or sell. The exercise of the option is, therefore, subject to the price stipulations.

The prices are usually predetermined by the platform operator. Various prices can be listed as available on the market for the same expiry of a certain class of options. Usually, prices depend on the value of the underlying share value. If the value of the underlying prices increases, the exercise prices also increase commensurately. The need to offer a range of prices for the same option contract is in order to suit the market conveniences of buyers of the contracts. The buyer can better match their own expectations of the pricing of the underlying shares in view of the position of their option contract. The exercise prices can also be varied in the course of an active contract when market dynamics dictate that such a move has to be made.

Premium

This is the value of the option that is usually expressed as a price that has to be paid by the option taker. Of the five features of options trading, this is the only one that is not determined by the platform operator. Usually, the premium prices are stated in cents corresponding to the value per share. To get the premium that has to be paid, for an option that is of relatively standard size, a formula is set. One has to take the premium price that has been stipulated on the option contract and multiply by the sum of the shares that a contract has.

For example, when the cost of a premium has been quoted as 16 cents. This has to be multiplied by the standard shares for every option, which is 100. This brings the payable premium for the option to $16.00. For an index option, there is another formula that offers a modality of calculating the premium. Index options have a standard multiplier index of $10. The quoted premium is therefore multiplied by this index multiplier to result to the total payable premium.

Having exercised the rights under an option contract, there are guidelines with regard to being eligible to vote and to earn dividends from the shares. The buyer in the case of a call option does not gain express rights to earn dividends on the shares. One has to wait until the exercised right of purchase is affected by the transfer of the shares. The same applies to vote rights. Usually, shares represent a voice in the company invested in. however; the voting rights also wait or the transfer of the shares to the buyer.

Similarly, the seller or writer in the put option does not expressly acquire the right to vote and earn dividends. One waits until the underlying assets, securities, or shares are transferred. This helps to create a structure of transfer of shareholding and transfer of the same. Any disputes about the expired contract have to be resolved, and proper registration of buying and selling be done for the holding trading the shares or asset.

Adjustments to Option Contracts

There is a general effort to ensure that option contracts are entered in under conditions that are standardized to the greatest extent possible. However, some market forces may upset the set optimum conditions and specifications. This may call or the making of some adjustments for the purpose of ensuring the preservation of the value attached to the positions of the various options contracts that have been entered into by various takers and writers.

In making the adjustments, it has to be established the kind of upset that has been caused on the market. Usually, it may affect one or more components of the options market. Identifying the affected components is necessary so that the adjustment is specific and particular to the kind of area of trading affected.

ASX, as one of the platform operators, has its rules that try to retain a tentatively predictable and standardized environment of trade. However, it also provides guidelines for the kind of measures that have to be made when adjustments are required. Conventions that guide the process of adjustment cushion participants on this kind of market and also protect takers and writers from arbitrary actions that may be unfavorable.

Options Pricing Fundamentals

When one is considering participating in options trading, certain aspects of this market are fundamental to consider. One is the premium and how it is calculated. This has been discussed earlier under the components of options trading. However, option premiums usually vary based on different factors that may affect them directly. The most important is the value of the share that underlies the particular option. The remainder of the time before the option also times out is also a determining. Option premium has two parts that comprise its total value. Intrinsic value is the first part and is followed by the time value.

Intrinsic value

This is the value as a result of calculating the difference between the exercise price that is quoted for a certain option trade and the market value the underlying asset over which options trading has been applied. This calculation should be a constant and be valid at any time of the life span of the contract. This will expose the motivation behind entering an options contract for the particular option. The intrinsic value of an option is usually important since it does not vary much and is not impacted upon by market forces or other external factors.

Time Value

This refers to the pressure that time exerts on a particular option as the life span progresses. It is important to analyze the market forces for the mere reason that times may get better to lead to an increase in the value of the option in the course of the period before the expiry of the option. One, therefore, has to be willing to pay to ensure that one takes advantage of an option whose value has gone high in the course of time.

Usually, there is a period when an option is at its most profitable stage. This is the time when one should consider buying the option and hence should always prepare for this time. Some options that do not have high intrinsic value may also have high time value if they are subject to market forces. However, they also pose a high risk of losses. The rate of decay of time value is not constant and may not be calculated mathematically. However, the rate of decay accelerates towards the end of the life span of the option.

Chapter 2: How to Start Options Trading

Appreciate That Options Trading Is Not Simple

It is vital at this stage to recapitulate the meaning of options trading. This is a contract that grants one the right of either buying or selling a security based on the speculative value of it in a limited period of time. However, the contract is not obligatory in nature. In understanding options trading, two forms of it have to be understood; first is a call option, and the other is the put option. The two are opposites of each other. One buys the former option when one expects an asset's value to go up over time but before the deadline of expiry of the contract expires. This allows one to buy an asset at a relatively lower price. The latter is the opposite entailing buying the right to exercise sell of an asset if one speculates that price of the asset would go down in the period before the expiry of the contract.

However, participating in this market requires one to have enough understanding of how it works. Any venture requires one to learn enough. Educating oneself generally about investment is the best standing point. This creates understanding and ensures that one is able to comprehend the way that the options trading market as an investment venture works.

Among the reasons why people should educate themselves on options trading is because it does not work in certain ways. It also does not have guarantees of profit. This means that it, just like other ventures, involves risks that should be understood. The risks in the case of trading options are quite extreme. It requires calculation and being accurate as one speculates about the drop and rising of the value of the options on offer. Being interest in a venture that involves a high-risk level requires enough knowledge and sometimes mentorship by those who have prior knowledge and understanding of the market in order to avoid plunging into frustration and wastage of capital.

One of the motivating aspects of trading options is that it allows one to capitalize on the advantage of leverage. Leverage is the means by which one can use the low capital investment to guarantee profits; all is not sweet and sugar. Essentially, options have underlying assets of greater value that it controls. However, one can edge into the potential purchase of this asset or acquisition of the underlying shares and the advantages that it comes with at a relatively affordable rate. However, the period for capitalizing the leverage is limited as there is a predetermined date, and the life span of the rights that have to be exercised expire. This may lead to losses.

In understanding options trading, the exact manner of risk has to be clear to one. The purchase of options is speculative, and this can be done as a cushion against incurring losses. When traders are able to make speculative purchases, it sets them up to potentially making huge returns. However, this is a gamble as one has to be accurate with the way they comprehend and predict the market forces, patterns, and trends. Predictions have to be accurate about the magnitude, the timing, and influences that impact on the price and value of the underlying asset. However, it puts the traders liable to potentially huge losses and has to content with incurring trade commissions that are usually quite high. Novice traders should get it right that options trading is more or less like a gamble, and risks are invaluable high. However, they are not prohibitively high as some have ventured into this market and have found some good level of success.

However, the options have been used, as opposed to making huge returns in profit, to protect people's stock investments. This is particularly the case with the put option that entails one putting one's shares up for sale in fear of an imminent drop of the share prices on the market. This way of using options has turned out safer and better in cushioning people against losses since one only forfeits the price of the contract.

Read and Understand Essential Literature Available On Options Trading

Reading is part of the process of educating one's self in business. A lot of literature is currently available on various platforms for the benefit of those seeking to understand investments and avenues of investment. Success and failure stories are also hugely available, particularly on the internet where people could acquire first-hand accounts on the options trading venture.

However, reading is only helpful if the correct material is being read. Not every account of business success stories is true. Some are exaggerated while others are written to arouse interest to influence people into making certain decisions for business purposes. The internet is full of hidden business activities, some of which are even hidden behind the sensational headlines of the literature resources striking people's eyes on their phones and computers. This means that knowledge is only good when it comes from the correct source.

There is a booklet that has reliable and valid information for those seeking understanding. It is entitled "Characteristics and Risks of Standardized Options."

This book is a comprehensive detail of just about everything that needs to be known about options trading. It is not written for other interest other than to expose the real mechanics of the trading and how it functions particularly at its most complicated level. It complies with the regulations of SEC, and it is usually distributed by the firms that operate in brokerage in this sector. It is usually issued to those who express interest to participate in trading by opening accounts for options trading. In the booklet, there is a better exposition of the concepts that apply in this industry and as well list the various available options trade classes that one could try out.

It also explains concepts of exercising spelling out how the taxman relates with options trading for the purpose of comprehension of the entire options-trade venture. It also considers the associated risks to ensure that readers are beware of the venture they are setting themselves up to join. If one has an interest in options trading, this is a must have read as one remains vigilant about some wrong information particularly by dubious brokers and businessmen who may mislead with an inaccurate representation of the trade.

Acquire an Understanding of the Basics of the Kinds of Trades

The kinds of trades have been discussed already. The trades are basically either a call option or the put option. These have to be understood well since they are the start of knowing this trade as an investment. The types of trade are the core part of the knowledge that a person can gain on options trading. All these can be explained with a desire to gain an understanding of how each of the two types of trades works. This can be achieved the desire for understanding can involve seeking mentorship or seeking consultancy firm. It can call for some level of schooling in order to begin to attain literacy, especially for those people who did not have prior knowledge of economic investments.

Having understood some of the concepts, one should internalize them. This is by reflecting on what has been learned so far about options trading and starting to view oneself as a potential expert who can even teach others. The way to do this is by, for instance, examining oneself on the understanding of the concepts. Some consultants have advised beginners to create a spreadsheet containing the various concepts and terms that are of the essence in understanding options trading. The terminologies have to be clearly stated in a way that does not obscure meaning.

Some of the important terms have already been explained in the initial chapter. However, the following terms are still vital in the understanding of option trading;

- Holder refers to a person who purchases an options trade.
- Writer is a term for the seller of the options trade.

Strike price that is also referred to as the exercise price is the amount that has to be paid for the purchase or sale of a security

– in this case depending on whether the trade is of the call or put type. A stick needs to go above or below the strike price, depending on the option type, in order for a profit to be registered on the purchased option.

Date of expiry is the deadline by which the rights in an option have to be exercised to either buy or sell share or the underlying security. After this date, the rights contained in the options trade are lost.

"In the money' is a term employed to indicate whether a market price, as compared to the strike price, is lower or higher. This helps to indicate whether the option is a call or put when it is higher than it is a call, and it is a put when "in the money" is lower.

"Out of the money" is the same concept as "in the money" only that it denotes the converse. It shows that in the case of a call, the underlying asset's market price is lower as compared to the exercise price. In the case of a put, "out of the money" refers to a state where the market price is higher as compared to the strike price. This means that "out of the money" implies a loss while "in the money" implies a profit.

These terms are, therefore, a vital part of understanding options trading. As it is, this trade has its own jargon and can, on the outset appear unattractive. The complexity of it is only represented by the appearance of the language that describes it.

For people who may not be so much interested in options trading, they get exhausted right at the stage of hearing these terms. Extra efforts have to be made to develop a body of knowledge first in order to forge a path to understanding.

Brokerage Account

Having understood how the trade works, it becomes essential to set up a brokerage where one can start creating a portfolio of transactions. As with anything about this venture, one has to know what it is they are going for when opening an account for brokerage. This is in order to ensure that nothing happens in the process of setting up an account that can later cause regret. Sometimes failures in investment can be traced back to just a single mistake along the way.

By understanding everything in opening a brokerage, one has to consider various factors that have an influence on the trade. First is to mind about the commissions that brokerages impose on the trading of various types of options. This is because it is an investment and one have to scout for the best deal that does not deal so much of expenses that impede value generation.

When one does not have the requisite knowledge on what the commission rates signify, it is based to seek interpretations. A brokerage should not obscure one from what is going on with the option trade. One has to be able to attain conversance with everything in the industry and ensure that he is able to seek all clarifications. As a matter of fact, one has to go in and research on the track record of the brokerages in order to shortlist those that are likely to best suit one's conveniences and trade interests.

One has to be alert for scammers and brokerages that are likely to give a raw deal. Some may want to take advantage of the ignorance and lack of technical knowledge of trading to exploit unsuspecting buyers and sellers. It is, in fact, necessary that trust is based less on persuasion and more the track record of the brokerage. It should be reputable, and a referred one is better. Only after thorough research is concluded and all reservations allayed that one should take a step to make any money transfers or deposits. Any brokerage with reported negative reviews and complaints of fraud should be avoided by all means.

In order to start trading options, it requires one to secure approval of the brokerage. Approvals depend on certain standards of merit. Some set thresholds of deposits in a brokerage account in order to give approval. The experience of the holder is also considered in order to ensure that those who are approved to start buying and selling know exactly what they are doing. Covered calls cannot be written if there is no account for options trading exists. Additionally, brokerages houses want to be sure that the risks that are related to the sector are well understood in order to give the green light to proceed.

Comprehending Technical Analysis

Options are usually limited by time due to the expiry date that is one of the conditions inhering this type of trading. They are, hence, short-term and have a life span. This means one is analyzing how prices for the underlying asset are behaving on the market with the intention to know when to exercise the rights in a bought option. This is for the purpose of ensuring that a profit margin is secured by all means possible. It is also to ensure that a healthy return on the invested capital through the purchase of an option is guaranteed. However, understanding the mechanics of price variations on the market in light of the desired profit margin that one is targeting one has to learn about technical analysis.

One has to educate themselves about the steadiness of market performance. Support and resistance levels of the market are to be studied in view of this. This is with regard to the level of performance that is relatively optimum on the market and which stock usually can neither go beyond or below. The lowest point is the support level, while the highest level is the resistance level. Usually, the support level is understood by studying historical trends of purchase to identify the level at which most purchases of an asset were purchased over time. The resistance level points at the value levels expressed as price, at which high sales of an asset or underlying security registered over time.

It is also vital to appreciate the significance of volume on the patterns of trading and price movements. In this regard, it refers to the movement of a stock in a certain direction of market performance that may be an indicator of profitability. This can be read as an opportunity to exercise rights or otherwise the "in the money" phenomenon. However, this is usually speculative, and accuracy depends on the experience and level of expertise in technical analysis of the options-trading forces.

It is also vital to be able to study chart patterns and make sense of them. Usually, these are based on the cliché that history repeats itself. Certain environmental phenomena usually result in predictable market response. High investment levels in the country, for instance, is an indicator of better stock price performance. Tax policies and how they are reviewed also relate to corresponding market behavior that may have been experienced from the past. This being said, it means that someone has to develop a love for studying graphs and going into historical economics in order to boost the development of intuition of reading trends that are telling of market performance.

Moving averages also are part of the knowledge that has to be learned in the interest of boosting technical analysis abilities. These averages usually are watched as they are the triggers of hope or doom. They are predictors of how the market will also behave either constantly or if there will be a lot of variations in the behavior of the market. Making sense of these also comes with experience in the trading industry in order to relate what they indicate. Once this has been learned, it will be easier to detect signals that determine decisions that have to be made with regard to the purchase of options.

Start Slow by Making Trials

In starting paper trading, one sets off by "paper trading." This is avoiding the habit of throwing caution at the wind and assuming that one has learned enough about the trade to start risking. Options trading requires one only to commit risk money that one is likely not to be hurt badly if they lose. One cannot commit money that they have labored much to earn to a venture whose technique of trade one has just learned. Paper trading requires one to test the waters with one leg by practicing and seeing how things go. One has to start slow, worrying out with little for a period of some months before they can really judge if they are acquiring the required experience and knowledge to handle the trading.

There is a way even to pretend. This can be done through software meant for practicing traders. Returns have to be observed for a streak of a few months, and when realized that the trend is returning well, one can then start to plunge into actual options trading gradually. The advantage of paper trading is that it is some form of fooling around that is done objectively for the purpose of seasoning and familiarization. It does not have the psychological weight that would otherwise be felt with actual trading when one is just starting trading. It helps to learn how trading works, to correlate the factors that influence the trading, and to enable one put into practice some of the knowledge gained while educating oneself about options trading.

Even in the trials, one has to try to be calculative with the capital to plow in. As already stated, this is a highly risky venture, and a learner cannot fully bear taking losses that he cannot understand how they were incurred. One should also adopt limit orders; this is by not purchasing options at their market prices since the price of executing them may turn out to be higher than one had anticipated. One has to determine how much they want to purchase options in order to capitalize on leverage.

Chapter 3: Platforms and Tools for Options Trading

A vital aspect of options trading is the platform that one uses to trade. This is because options trading requires monitoring and requires a continuous analysis of trends. Performance is also monitored, and since the trade is impacted upon by a complex of factors, one has to choose a suitable platform for trading.

A good platform for trading should offer a lot of opportunities for traders. These are opportunities to orient beginners into trading, development for the existing ones, and actualization for those with a record on the platform. A platform of trading should also prescribe the available products and any resources that subscribers on the platform can benefit from to push themselves to profitability.

With the technology developing at high speed, platforms continue to improve by the day. This is both complicating the trading itself as well as providing avenues of spreading awareness about the business. A platform should, therefore, have the ability to offer the best possible experience for the traders to do trade and grow both in experience and returns without meeting a lot of platform limitations and frustrations.

A Platform Takes Trading To the Holders

Trading involves a lot of complexities that may sometimes be scary. It makes people lose interest as soon as they develop it. They perceive it as too complicated. The impression is that it is a venture meant for the people who have higher comprehension of concepts in the economics specialty and that those who do not a background in this area will have difficulty getting on board.

However, a trading platform has to present options trading as a venture that is possible and in which anyone with interest can succeed in. The days when options trading and any other forms of trading were presented as a show of sophistication are long gone. In this era, every sector of investment is being portrayed as possible, and businesses are now being made easier in order to create a better chance for people to dare. A platform that limits investment so much and is exclusive in terms of how it carries out its trading activities is irrelevant to modern economic patterns.

Platforms, therefore, have to be interactive and user-friendly. They should have the ability to encourage users to feel like they can handle the trade. It should also have the capability to gauge the level of use and give feedback about how well they are able to use it. If it is a website, for instance, it has to be able to report the numbers as people visit it and how many eventually end up creating accounts and trading. Counting traffic is essential for feedback that can lead to the creation of a better experience for the users.

Competition

The reason for considering a good platform is because the competition is high today. Competition has led to the creation of better trading experiences through innovation. Platforms are now trying to out-do each other in being the avenues of options trading. They are doing this by striving to create ways of improving user experience. It is therefore essential to identify the various parameters of comparing the platforms. Eventually, one has to choose a platform that offers optimal access to the trading world.

In choosing a platform sometimes, one would want to take advantage of the advantages of different platforms. This is looking at one's style of trading and how they wish to monitor their business and see if a platform is more transparent in handling the tares or whether it offers a clear lens of controlling purchases and sells of options. This is the reason why the various platforms have to be assessed in terms of their potential. Usually, platforms are related to the tools of trading. Some of the tools of trading can be found right on the platform of trading.

When a platform of trading also has various tools of aiding trading, it ensures that one can gain a lot of benefits at one place. This makes the platform a utility platform where a person can visit for more purposes than just trading. It also makes it better. For instance, if a platform has videos that offer trading tutorials. This can make it resourceful in imparting competency in participating in the very sector that the platform operates.

To best benefit from competition, one has to understand the type of trade they want to do. This is by naming their price and gauging which platform can serve better in ensuring returns and value generation. This is in order to avoid going into trading in desperation, and one has to be patient to see if the platform can also come out and meet a trader at their point of ability and also help in trading in comfort where risk is at a minimum.

Types of Trading Platforms

There are various platforms in options trading that one could consider. There is web-based trading that utilizes the power of the search engines. This platform has many operators since the building of websites in the modern age is easy. This platform is responsible for the growth in the popularity of options trading. People can trade from anyone, open brokerage accounts, make deposits, and participate in the buying and selling of assets in the comfort of their homes.

With the presence of a lot of technological gadgets such as smartphones, tablets, and computers, web-based trading has been easy and possible. Websites can be built with additional resources for learning and tools that can be an advantage for both novice and seasoned traders. On the websites, regular updates on the market can be posted to keep traders informed about trends, patterns, and even help in analyzing price movements for the subscribers.

The web is also a good platform when it comes to filtering opportunities and options based on suitability and preference in view of the various abilities of users. They can be designed to be customizable even when the options markets are standardized.

User Friendliness

Usually, websites are good as they offer various tools that aid beginners to edge into trading options. ASX, for example, offers a variety of web-based resources that guide people in their efforts to understand trading. This includes online chats that have instant feedback as a team is dedicated to the work site for correspondence purposes. The aim of this is to offer motivation and impetus to go on with the discovery of the markets trends until one becomes a seasoned trader.

Friendliness is also in terms of the efforts that are made to create peer assistance. This is through creating groups of traders that influence each other and can learn from the vast experiences in the trading of the options. This can be a positive influence on the journey to gaining competence and help support an environment where people can relate and interact as they pursue their various financial goals.

It is important to consider the fact that some of the platforms of trading offer important tools that can be helpful in deciding on options. The tools are those that help in monitoring markets and simplify the technical analysis process for the trader. This can help one to sharpen their trading strategy to align well with the ultimate goal of trading. This depends on whether the goal of trading is to earn money in terms of profit or hedge oneself against losses on the underlying asset.

Tools to Learn

Upon mastering the various basics of trading and making the initial moves to start trading, one has to use various tools that help to indicate the advancers and decliners on the market. Greeks are some kind of metrics that those involved in options trading capitalize to ensure maximization of returns. These "Greeks" include the delta matrix that measures the correlation between price movements of the underlying asset relative to the price of the option. The tools for monitoring the movements for these parameters of trading are vital as everyone is always trading with a focus on minimizing losses while geared towards profit maximization.

The gamma is another tool that can help to predict market trends in order to do good timing for decisions on exercising rights in options. Gamma is an indicator of the rate of delta variations for the option price as compared to the asset price. This goes hand in hand with the time-decay tool that indicators the value movement, either upwards or downwards, in the period of life options. This helps to signal which options to avoid given the remaining time of the life span and the value implications thereon.

There is also the aspect of the volatility of the asset underlying a particular option trade. Some of the assets or stocks do not have inherent volatility to appreciate in value due to their nature. Assets that have high market volatility usually gain a lot on the market, and hence, the value behaves better to favor the call option trade. Products with ugh volatility and high inherent value are not suitable for the put option trade since they will occasion a loss. It is therefore important to use correct tools that aid in the analysis if the technical mechanics of the options trading business.

Tools are not just concrete things that can be manipulated. Some tools, especially in trading, are conceptual in nature. This is because they are the ones by which one can trade and aid in decision making. They sample out market forces and help in mapping out market trends for the benefit of the trader. To perceive tools as only concrete in nature is a misconception of the whole options trading venture.

Professional level platforms

There is a level in trading where one attains sophistication and attains the intuition to thrive in options trading regardless of the ways market forces seem to behave. At this level, someone needs tools that can help them edge into the horizon of complexity in trading. The platforms for this professional level exist, and they have to offer tools that are an edge above the basic level. These tools have to offer strategies of competing to control the stocks and rise above the market forces. At this level, one becomes daring, and the possibilities that the platform offers should only be dared by those who have mastered trading and are sure of beating odds as they speculate about squeezing out value form trades that otherwise be perceived as highly risky.

The platform should be full of idea probing resources that lead one to gain the courage to trade more and more. Web-based platforms of this level include the think or swim platform that is categorically for seasoned traders. This is the reason why one has to know the platform to trade on based on their level of experience in options trading. Some platforms are too complicated for the starters. The tools are even out of the capacity of a beginner to comprehend the trades appear to have higher risks that may wipe away hard-earned fortunes.

Mobile Trading

Some platforms have taken advantage of the handiness of the mobile era. These entail the smartphone lifestyle and the flashier iPod, iPad, and tablet culture. This is when trading is being placed in the palms of traders to hold and run away with it. This platform usually targets traders that want to capitalize on device optimization. This is the reason why trades have classes. Some of the options could be device targeted as they can only be taken advantage of when one using the suitable device for trading, provided the relevant support tools that the device offers.

Mobile trading also comes in order to keep people abreast. This is because opportunities sometimes appear and disappear on people because they are not using a device that enables them to be precise and timely in decision making and action.

With mobile trading, apps have been developed, some with notification capability. One can customize the apps to ensure that no opportunity comes that is not taken advantage of. Opportunities' in trading have to be seized and relying on a platform that is less handy and far means that opportunities of trading are lost.

What Are We Looking For In Platforms And Tools?

First is the opportunity to learn. There is no worse platform of trading than that which targets only to admit traders who do not understand what they are getting into. The education that a platform has to offer should be free as trading is itself risky enough to prohibit any extra expenses in the process. Platform operators should understand that any interested person who visits their platform is a potential subscriber, and they should freely offer support to educate them for the purpose of acquisition of requisite knowledge on options trading.

Some of the platforms have gone as opening structures units for education on options trading. These courses are taken online, and coaching is done through the provision of a stream of webinars transmitted live or uploading recorded ones. This is for platforms that appreciate that trading is an informed gamble that requires one to know enough. They even test the proficiency of understanding trading concepts and mechanics for the purpose of ensuring that any people who trade on the platform are doing what they understand to build the platform ratings.

It is also vital for a starter to set standards that the broker's customer service should pass. In trading, brokers should work enough to earn the commission that they charge on the options that subscribers trade on buy. This is because some brokers are obscure and may not involve the options trader who is buying options in decisions that directly impact on his capital. One, therefore, faces a lot of anxiety if the broker is not responsive and transparent on the particular mechanics that influence trade.

Excellent broker services try to suit customer needs. They ask options traders subscribed to their platform what their preferred means of reaching is. Whether a live chat or phone call suits the customer or not. They also dedicate a desk for trading communications and queries and has the discipline to listen to customers and their issues with patience. They, in fact, have feedback on the quality of customer service that those who reach out get.

Software Trading Platforms

These are more complex than web-based ones. This is because they are run on the trader's computer, and the trader is required to understand what the software does and interpret it. Even when the brokerage can offer assistance, software-based platforms require the trader to have enough technical know how to read charts, graphs, and understand patterns that represent various components of options trading.

For beginners, a complex platform has to be avoided by all means. This is because one is bound to engage in aspects of trading that they do not have an understanding of. A trading platform simply has to be simple and clear. The interface should not be too busy as to scare away those traders who are not accustomed. This is the reason why operators usually separate the platforms that as designed for basic use, which is suitable for novices, and advanced trading for the seasoned ones.

Then a broker has to offer a tutorial that guides the user on how to navigate their platform. Everything has to be explained, even those that one would deem to be obvious. Screenshots can even be available in order to be categorical and emphatic. This ensures that a broker has offered all possible assists for the trader to benefit from the offers and products on the platform successfully.

Cost Implication

It is important for the trader to know that some brokers may have charges attached to some of the services, resources, and tools that they provide on their platform. These have to be assessed in terms of their worth and whether the costs are necessary. Making some tolls premium may be an indicator of quality but not always. This is particularly the case when other platforms provide similar services toll-free.

Screening tools are particularly the ones that are bound to attract charges because they have abilities to analyze and assess market trends. They can do the thinking for the trader and help him in decision making. One has to read about the specifications of the tools and ascertain what they or cannot do. This is in order to know if they are customizable for the purpose of serving the needs and conveniences of traders.

Some charges can even be attached to the quotes update feed. Usually, the quotes can be accessed in real time for those who want to see them in real time. The quotes are important in influencing idea generation and sometimes can tip people of opportunities in the market. There is usually a delay for those who access the quotes updates for free.

It is also vital to understand platforms do not provide all the tools to everyone using their platform to trade. Some of the cutting-edge tools that can best serve the business interests of traders are premium. They have subscription charges or otherwise only appear on the accounts of traders who constantly sustain a certain threshold of account balance minimums. This is particularly the case for platforms that operate at the professional level. They require one to be active and remain active in trading since this serves the business interests of the brokerage through the commissions it earns on options contracts. In return, it offers the consultancy, expertise, and resource repository for one to realize value out of the options trades. This is why they attach a price on some of the tools.

Final Thoughts

One can only trust a platform that has a reputation for efficiency. This is a platform that ensures orders have a quick span of execution. This particularly for traders who understand the benefits of entering quick and instantly exiting from offered positions. The charges of platform subscription also matter. This is whether they are monthly or per year. It is vital to understand the way of earning waivers on platform fees. It could be through ensuring compliance with balance minimums or activity of trades per a set span of time.

Chapter 4: Financial Leverage

Leverage is a concept that is used by both companies and investors. For investors, the notion of leverage is used to try and increase returns that come on investment. To use leverage, you have to make use of various instruments, including future, options, and margin accounts.

The use of leverage n options trading helps boost your profits. Trading in options can give you huge leverage and allow you to generate huge profits from a small investment.

Definition

Leverage is the ability to trade a large number of options using just a small amount of capital. Many traders feel that leverage is, but studies have found that the risk in leveraged options is nearly the same to non-leveraged securities.

Why Is Leverage Riskier?

Trading options using leverage is usually considered riskier because it exaggerates the potential of the business. For instance, you can use $500 to enter a trade that has a potential of $7000. Remember the first rule of trading – don't trade what you cannot lose.

This isn't as true as it seems, which is why it is vital that you know what you are doing at all times.

Leverage makes you utilize capital more efficiently. For this reason, many traders love the trade because it allows them to go for larger positions with limited capital.

When you use leverage, you don't reduce the potential profit that you will gain; rather, you reduce the risk in certain trades. For instance, if you want to put your money in 10,000 options at $8 per share, you would need to risk $80,000 worth of investment. This means that the whole amount of $80,000 would be at risk. However, you can use leverage to place a smaller amount of money, thus reducing the risk of loss.

This is the way you need to look at leverage, which is the right way.

Before you can trade leverage, you need to find a way to maximize the gains in each trade. Here are a few tips that you can explore:

Know When to Run

You need to cut losses early enough and then let your winning trades run to completion. Just the way you run other trades; you need to know when to cut your losses so that you don't end up bankrupt. You need to make use of stop losses when running leverage in trades.

Have a Stop Loss Set

As a trader, you need to determine your stop loss set so that you don't lose more than you can afford. The set that you come up with will depend upon the situation of the market at any time. Whatever the case, always make sure you have a set to guide you.

Don't Go With the Trade

Many traders try to chase a trade to the finish, something that ends up discouraging them and making them lose money. Once a move happens, you need to accept and wait for the next opening. Always be patient because just like the other opportunity came *along, another one will definitely come by*.

Have Limit Orders

Instead of placing market limits, opt for limit orders instead so that you can save on fees. The limit orders also help you reign in your emotions when you trade.

Learn About Technical Analysis

Make sure you learn about technical analysis before you jump into trading. Technical analysis will make sure you have the information that you need to make decisions fast.

The Advantages of Leverage in Options Trading

When you use leverage, you increase your financial capability as a trader and enjoy better trading results. You can change the amount of leverage at your discretion. This is because when you open a trading account, you have all the power of managing the amount of capital that you place on a trade. The good news is that you can use leverage free of charge, but you need to make sure you know how it works and whether it will work for you or not.

The level of leverage varies. Some trading platforms offer leverage from as low as 1:1 up to and beyond 1:1000. As a trader, it is advisable that you go for the largest leverage possible so that you can make the biggest returns.

Another advantage is that low leverage allows you as a new trader to survive. When starting out in options trading, you have the capacity to make small trades with little to show for your efforts. With leverage, you can make use of leverage to place trades that run into thousands of dollars without risking the same amount in terms of investment. As long as you know what you are doing, you have the capability to enjoy massive profits.

Disadvantages of Leverage in Options Trading

As much as it is a good way to make huge profits, you also need to understand that leverage comes with many demerits. These include:

Magnifies the Losses

With leverage, you will be faced with huge losses if the trade decides to go the other way. And since the original outlay is way smaller than what you end up losing, many traders forget that they are placing their capital at risk. Make sure you come up with a ratio that will help protect your interests and then know how to manage trade risk.

No Privileges

When you use leverage to trade, you sacrifice full ownership of the asset. For instance, when you use leverage, you give up the opportunity of enjoying dividends. This is because the amount on the dividend is deducted from the account regardless of the position of the trade.

Margin Calls

A margin call is when the lender asks you to add funds so that you keep the trade open. You have to decide whether you wish to add funds or exit a position to reduce the exposure.

Incur Expenses

When you use leverage to trade options, you will receive the money from the lender so that you can use the full position. Most traders opt to keep their positions open overnight, which attracts a fee to cover the costs.

How Much Leverage Do You Need in Options Trading

Knowing how to trade options needs detailed knowledge about the various aspects of economics. For many people, the lack of knowledge to use leverage is the major cause of losses.

Studies show that many traders who opt for options lose money in the process. This happens whether for smaller or high leverage.

Risks of High Leverage

In options trading, the capital for placing a trade is usually sourced from a broker. While you have the ability to borrow huge amounts to place on a trade, you can gain more if the trade is successful.

A few years back, traders were able to offer leverages of up to 400 times the initial capital. However, rules and regulations have been, and at the moment, you can only access 50 times what you have. For instance, if you have $1000, you can control up to $50,000.

Choosing the Right Leverage

You need to look at different factors when choosing the kind of leverage that will work for you.

First, you need to start with low levels of leverage, because the more you borrow, the more you will need to pay back. Second, you need to use stops to make sure you protect the amount you have borrowed. Remember losses won't go down well with you.

All in all, you need to choose leverage which you find is comfortable for you. If you are a beginner, go for low leverage so that you minimize risks. If you know what you are doing, then go for maximum leverage to build your returns.

Using stops on order allows you to reduce loses when the trade changes direction. As a newbie, this is the only protection you need to make it in the market. This is because you will learn about the trades and how to place them while limiting any losses that might arise.

How to Manage Risk in Options Trading

Options trading comes with a number of risks that you need to manage so that you can enjoy the profits and minimize losses.

Here are a few risks and how to deal with them.

Losing More than What You Have

This risk is inherent in options trading, especially if you are using leverage to make a trade. It means that you put up a small fraction of the initial deposit to open the trade. This means that your fate is in the hands of the direction of the market. If it goes along with your prediction, you will gain more than the deposit. On the other hand, if the direction changes and you lose the position, you might end up losing more than your initial deposit.

When this happens, you need to have a strategy in place to help mitigate the risk. What you need to do in this case is to set a limit, so that you define the exact level at which the trade should stop so that you don't lose more than you can handle.

Positions Closing Unexpectedly

When positions close unexpectedly, they lead to loss of money. To keep the trades open, you need to have some money in the account. This aspect is called the margin, and if you don't have enough funds to cover the margin, then the position might close.

To mitigate this, you need to keep an eye on the running balances and always add funds as needed.

Sudden Huge Losses or Gains

The market can turn out to be volatile, and when it does, you need to move fast. Markets change depending on the news or something else in the market, which can be an announcement, event, or changes in trader behavior.

Apart from having stops, you also need to get notifications regarding any upcoming movement, which tells you whether to react or not,

Orders Filled in Erroneously

When you give instructions to a broker to place a trade for you, and the broker instead does the opposite. This is termed slippage. When this happens, use guaranteed stops to make sure you protect yourself against any slippage that might occur.

How to Trade Smarter Using Leverage

Even with leverage in tow, you need to have a way to trade better. With many mistakes occurring during a trade, you stand to lose more than gain if you don't have the right tips to excel. Let us look at the top mistakes that you go through to get to the top.

Misunderstanding Leverage

Many beginners don't understand leverage and go ahead to misuse this feature, barely realizing the risk they are exposing themselves to.

To make this work for you, learn about leverage, and master it. Understand what it is and what it isn't and then find out the best ways to make use of it. You also need to understand how much you can put in without running huge losses.

Having No Exit Plan

Just like socks, you need to control your emotions when trading options. It doesn't mean that you have to swallow your greed and fear; rather, you need to have a plan that you can go with. Once you have a plan, you need to stick to it so that even when things aren't going your way, you have something to guide you to make a recovery.

You need to have an exit plan, which means you know when to drop a trade.

Failure to Try New Strategies

You need to make sure you try out a few new strategies depending on the level of trading you want to achieve. Most traders get a single strategy and then stick to it even when it is not working out for them. When this happens, you are often tempted to go against the rules that you set down.

Maintain an open mind so that you can learn new option trading strategies to help you get more out of your trades.

Chapter 5: The Basics of Technical Analysis

Technical analysis is the method of using charts and other recording methods to analyze various data in options trading. Using these visual instruments, you have the chance to determine the direction of the market because they give you a trend.

This method focuses on studying the supply and demand of a market. The price will be seen to rise when the investor realizes the market is undervalued, and this leads to buying. If they think that the market is overvalued, the prices will start falling, and this is deemed the perfect time to sell.

You need to understand the movement of the various indicators to make the perfect decision. This method works on the premise that history usually repeats itself – a huge change in the prices affects the investors in any situation.

History

Technical analysis has been used over the years in trades. The technical analysis methods have been used for over a hundred years to come up with deductions regarding the market.

In Asia, the use of technical analysis led to the development of candlestick techniques, and it forms the main charting techniques.

Over time, more tools and techniques have come up to help traders come up with predictions of the prices in various markets.

There are many indicators that you can use to determine the direction of the market, but only a few are valuable to your course. Let us look at the various indicators and how to use them.

Support and Resistance

These levels occur at points where both the buyer and the seller aren't dormant. These levels are displayed on the chart using a horizontal line extended in the past to the future.

The different prices reach at the support and resistance points in the future.

How to Apply Support and Resistance

• Using these points allows you to know when to call or put.

• Support and resistance give you a way to determine the entry point to use for a directional trade.

The Significance of Trends in Option Trading

Technical analysis works on the premise of the trend. These trends come by due to the interaction of the buyer and the seller. The aggressiveness of one of the parties in the market will determine how steep the trend becomes. To make a profit, you have to take advantage of the changes in the price movement.

To understand the direction of the trend, you ought to look at the troughs and peaks and how they relate to each other.

When looking for money in options trading, you ought to trade with a trend. The trend is what determines the decision you make when faced with a situation – whether to buy or to sell. You need to know the various signs that a prevailing trend is soon ending so that you can manage the risks and exit the trades the right way.

Characteristics of Technical Analysis

This analysis makes use of models and trading rules using different price and volume changes. These include the volume, price, and other different market info.

Technical analysis is applied among financial professionals and traders and is used by many option traders.

The Principles of Technical analysis

Many traders on the market use the price to come up with information that affects the decision you make ultimately. The analysis looks at the trading pattern and what information it offers you rather than looking at drivers such as news events, economic and fundamental events.

Price action usually tends to change every time because the investor leans towards a certain pattern, which in turn predicts trends and conditions.

Prices Determine Trends

Technical analysts know that the price in the market determines the trend of the market. The trend can be up, down, or move sideways.

History Usually Repeats Itself

Analysts believe that an investor repeats the behavior of the people that traded before them. The investor sentiment usually repeats itself. Due to the fact that the behavior repeats itself, traders know that using a price pattern can lead to predictions.

The investor uses the research to determine if the trend will continue or if the reversal will stop eventually and will anticipate a change when the charts show a lot of investor sentiment.

Combination with Other Analysis Methods

To make the most out of the technical analysis, you need to combine it with other charting methods on the market. You also need to use secondary data, such as sentiment analysis and indicators.

To achieve this, you need to go beyond pure technical analysis, and combine other market forecast methods in line with technical work. You can use technical analysis along with fundamental analysis to improve the performance of your portfolio.

You can also combine technical analysis with economics and quantitative analysis. For instance, you can use neural networks along with technical analysis to identify the relationships in the market. Other traders make use of technical analysis with astrology.

Other traders go for newspaper polls, sentiment indicators to come with deductions.

The Different Types of Charts Used in Technical Analysis

Candlestick Chart

This is a charting method that came from the Japanese. The method fills the interval between opening and closing prices to show a relationship. These candles use color coding to show the closing points. You will come across black, red, white, blue, or green candles to represent the closing point at any time.

Open-high-low-close Chart (OHLC)

These are also referred to as bar charts, and they give you a connection between the maximum and minimum prices in a trading period. They usually feature a tick on the left side to show the open price and one on the right to show the closing price.

Line Chart

This is a chart that maps the closing price values using a line segment.

Point and Figure Chart

This employs numerical filters that reference times without fully using the time to construct the chart.

Overlays

These are usually used on the main price charts and come in different ways:

• *Resistance* – refers to a price level that acts as the maximum level above the usual price

• *Support* – the opposite of resistance, and it shows as the lowest value of the price

• *Trend line* – this is a line that connects two troughs or peaks.

• *Channel* – refers to two trend lines that are parallel to each other

• *Moving average* – a kind of dynamic trendline that looks at the average price in the market

• *Bollinger bands* – these are charts that show the rate of volatility in a market.

• *Pivot point* – this refers to the average of the high, low, and closing price averages for a certain stock or currency.

Price-based Indicators

These analyze the price values of the market. These include:

• *Advance decline line* – this is an indicator of the market breadth

- *Average directional index* – shows the strength of a trend in the market

- *Commodity channel index* – helps you to identify cyclical trends in the market

- *Relative strength index* – this is a chart that shows you the strength of the price

- *Moving average convergence (MACD)* – this shows the point where two trend line converge or diverge.

- *Stochastic oscillator* – this shows the close position that has happened within the recent trading range

- *Momentum* – this is a chart that tells you how fast the price changes

The Benefits of Technical Analysis in Options Trading

There are a variety of benefits that you enjoy when you use technical analysis in trading options. The benefits arise from the fact that traders are usually asking a lot of questions touching on the price of the market and entry points. While the forecast for prices is a huge task, the use of technical analysis makes it easier to handle.

The major advantages of technical analysis include

Expert Trend Analysis

This is the biggest advantage of technical analysis in any market. With this method, you can predict the direction of the market at any time. You can determine whether the market will move up, down or sideways easily.

Entry and Exit Points

As a trader, you need to know when to place a trade and when to opt out. The entry point is all about knowing the right time to enter the trade for good returns. Exiting a trade is also vital because it allows you to reduce losses.

Leverage Early Signals

Every trader looks for ways to get early signals to assist them in making decisions. Technical analysis gives you signals to trigger a decision on your part. This is usually ideal when you suspect that a trend will reverse soon. Remember the time the trend reverses are when you need to make crucial decisions.

It Is Quick

In options trading, you need to go with techniques that give you fast results. Additionally, getting technical analysis data is cheaper than other techniques in fundamental analysis, with some companies offering free charting programs. If you are in the market to make use of short time intervals such as 1-minute, 5-minute, 30 minute or 1-hour charts, you can get this using technical analysis.

It Gives You A Lot of Information

Technical analysis gives you a lot of information that you can use to make trading decisions. You can easily build a position depending on the information you get then take or exit trades. You have access to information such as chart pattern, trends, support, resistance, market momentum, and other information.

The current price of an asset usually reflects every known information of an asset. While the market might be rife with rumors that the prices might surge or plummet, the current price represents the final point for all information. As the traders and investors change their bearing from one part to another, the changes in asset reflect the current value perception.

If all this turns out to be true, then the only info you require is a price chart that gives all the price reflections and predictions. There isn't any need for you to worry yourself with the reasons why the price is rising or falling when you can use a chart to determine everything.

With the right technical analysis information, you can make trading easier and faster because you make decisions based not on hearsay but facts. You don't have to spend your time reading and trying to make headway in financial news. All you need us to check what the chart tells you.

You Understand Trends

If the prices on the market were to gyrate randomly without any direction, you would find it hard to make money. While these trends run in all directions, the prices always move in trends. Directional bias allows you to leverage the benefits of making money. Technical analysis allows you to determine when a trend occurs and when it doesn't occur, or when it is in reversal.

Many of the profitable techniques that are used by the traders to make money follow trends. This means that you find the right trend and then look for opportunities that allow you to enter the market in the same direction as the trend. This helps you to capitalize on the price movement.

Trends run in various degrees. The degree of the trend determines how much money you make, whether in the short term or long-term trading. Technical analysis gives you all the tools that make it possible for you to do this.

History Always Repeats Itself

Technical analysis uses common patterns to give you the information to trade. However, you need to understand that history will not be exact when it repeats itself, though. The current analysis will be either bigger or smaller, depending on the existing market conditions. The only thing is that it won't be a replica of the prior pattern.

This pans out easily because most human psychology doesn't change so much, and you will see that the emotions have a hand in making sure that prices rise and fall. The emotions that traders exhibit create a lot of patterns that lead to changes in prices all the time. As a trader, you need to identify these patterns and then use them for trading. Use prior history to guide you and then the current price as a trigger of the trade.

Enjoy Proper Timing

Do you know that without proper timing you will not be able to make money at all? One of the major advantages of technical analysis is that you get the chance to time the trades. Using technical analysis, you get to wait, then place your money in other opportunities until it is the right time to place a trade.

Applicable Over a Wide Time Frame

When you learn technical analysis, you get to apply it to many areas in different markets, including options. All the trading in a market is based mostly on the patters that are as a result of human behavior. These patterns can then be mapped out on a chart to be used across the markets.

While there is some difference between analyzing different securities, you will be able to use technical analysis in most of the markets.

Additionally, you can use the analysis in any timeframe, which is applicable whether you use hourly, daily, or weekly charts. These markets are usually taken to be fractal, which essentially means that patterns that appear on a small scale will also be present on a large scale as well.

Technical Analysis Secrets to Become the Best Trader

To make use of technical analysis the right way, you need to follow time-testing approaches that have made the technique a gold mine for many traders. Let us look at the various tips that will take you from novice to pro in just a few days:

Use More than One Indicator

Numbers make trading easy, but it also applies to the way you apply your techniques. For one, you need to know that just because one technical indicator is better than using one, applying a second indicator is better than using just one. The use of more than one indicator is one of the best ways to confirm a trend. It also increases the odds of being right.

As a trader, you will never be 100 percent right at all times, and you might even find that the odds are stashed against you when everything is plain to see. However, don't demand too much from your indicators such that you end up with analysis paralysis.

To achieve this, make use of indicators that complement each other rather than the ones that clash against each other.

Go For Multiple Time Frames

Using the same buy signal every day allows you to have confidence that the indicator is giving you all you need to know to trade. However, make sure you look for a way to use multiple timeframes to confirm a trend. When you have a doubt, it is wise that you increase the timeframe from an hour to a day or from a daily chart to a weekly chart.

Understand that No Indicator Measures Everything

You need to know that indicators are supposed to show how strong a trend is, they won't tell you much more. So, you need to understand and focus on what the indicator is supposed to communicate instead of working with assumptions.

Go With the Trend

If you notice that an option is trading upward, then go ahead and buy it. Conversely when the trend stops trending, then it is time to sell it. If you aren't sure of what is going on in the market at that time, then don't make a move.

However, waiting might make you lose profitable trades as opposed to trading. You also miss out on opportunities to create more capital.

Have the Right Skills

It really takes superior analytical capabilities and real skill to be successful at trading, just like any other endeavor. Many people think that it is hard to make money with options trading, but with the right approach, you can make extraordinary profits.

You need to learn and understand the various skills so that you know what the market seeks from you and how to achieve your goals.

Trade with a Purpose

Many traders go into options trading with the main aim of having a hobby. Well, this way you won't be able to make any money at all. What you need to do is to trade for the money – strive to make profits unlike those who try to make money as a hobby.

Always Opt for High value

Well, no one tells you to trade any security that comes your way – it is purely a matter of choice. Try and go for high-value options so that you can trade them the right way. Make use of fundamental analysis to choose the best options to trade in.

Be Disciplined

When using technical analysis, you might find yourself in situations that require you to make a decision fast. To achieve success, you need to have strict risk management protocols.

Don't base on your track record to come up with choices; instead, make sure you follow what the analysis tells you.

Don't Overlook Your Trading Plan

The trading plan is in place to guide you when things go awry. Coming up with the plan is easy, but many people find it hard to implement the plan the right way. The trading plan has various components – the signals and the take-profit/stop-loss rules. Once you get into the market, you need to control yourself because you have already taken a leap. Remember you cannot control the indicators once they start running – all you can do is to prevent yourself from messing up everything.

Come up with the trading rules when you are unemotional to try and mitigate the effects of making bad decisions.

Accept Losses

Many people trade with one thing in mind – losses aren't part of their plan. This is a huge mistake because you need to understand that every trade has two sides to it – a loss and a profit. Remember that the biggest mistake that leads to losses isn't anything to do with bad indicators rather using them the wrong way. Always have a stop-loss order when you trade to prevent loss of money.

Have a Target When You Trade

So, what do you plan to achieve today? Remember, trading is a way to grow your capital as opposed to saving. Options trading is a business that has probable outcomes that you get to estimate. When you make a profit, make sure you take some money from the table and then put it in a safe place.

How to Apply Technical Analysis

Many traders have heard of technical analysis, but they don't know how to use it to make deductions and come up with decisions that impact their trades. Here are the different steps to make sure you have the right decision when you use technical analysis.

1. *Identify a Trend*

You need to identify an option and then see whether there is a trend or not. The trend might be driving the options up or down. The market is bullish if it is moving up and bearish when it is moving down. As a trader, you need to go along with the trend instead of fighting it. When you fight against the trend, you incur unnecessary losses that will make it hard to achieve the rewards that you seek.

You also need to have good ways to identify the trend; this is because the market has the capacity to move in a certain direction. It is not all about identifying the direction of the trend but also when the trend is moving out of the trend.

So, how can you identify a trend the right way? Here are some tools to use so as to get the right trend:

• Using triangles that map major swings

• The Bill Williams Fractals indicator helps you to identify the trend

- Use the moving average

- Trend lines give you an idea of the direction of the trend

Once you identify the trend, the next step is to try and mark the support and resistance levels

2. Support and Resistance Levels

You need to understand the support and resistance levels that are within the trend. Use the Fibonacci retracement tool to identify these spots on the trend.

3. Look for Patterns

Patterns need to show you what to expect in a certain market. You can use candlesticks to determine the chart pattern.

Chapter 6: Mindset: Controlling Your Emotions (Trading Psychology)

GBP/USD	82%	1.54260	14 15	▾	🕐 04:23
EUR/JPY	82%	135.365	14 15	▾	🕐 04:23
GBP/JPY	81%	183.543	14 15	▾	🕐 04:23
USD/JPY	73%	118.983	14 15	▾	🕐 04:23
USD/CAD	79%	1.25174	14 15	▾	🕐 04:23
USD/CHF	73%	0.94890	14 15	▾	🕐 04:23
EUR/GBP	78%	0.73751	14 15	▾	🕐 04:23
AUD/USD	79%	0.77801	14 15	▾	🕐 04:23
AUD/NZD	73%	1.03561	14 15	▾	🕐 04:23
NZD/USD	73%	0.75125	14 15	▾	🕐 04:23

Trading psychology is the mental state and emotions that determine the success or failure of trading options. It represents the aspect of your behavior that dictates the decisions you make when faced with a trade. The psychology is vital to any trade and can be compared to experience, knowledge, and skills in determining your success as a trader.

When you decide to start options trading, you need to grasp the concept of risk-taking and discipline that determine the implementation of any trade.

The two most common emotions are greed and fear, while others are regret and hope.

The Basics of Trading Psychology

We associate trading psychology to some behaviors and emotions that are often the triggers for catalysts for decisions. The most common emotions that every trader will come across is fear and greed.

Fear

At any given time, fear represents one of the worst kinds of emotions that you can have. Check in your newspaper one day, and you read about a steep selloff, and the next thing is trying to rack your brain about what to do next even if it isn't the right action at that time.

Many investors think that they know what will happen in the next few days, which makes them have a lot of confidence in the outcome of the trade. This leads to investors getting into the trade at a level that is too high or too low, which in turn makes them react emotionally.

As the trader puts a lot of hope on the single trade, the level of fear tends to increase, and hesitation and caution kick in.

Fear is part of every trader, but skilled traders have the capacity to manage the fear. There are various types of fears that you will experience, let us look at a few of them:

The Fear to Lose

Have you ever entered a trade and all you could think about is losing? The fear of losing makes it hard for you to execute the perfect strategy or enter or exit a strategy at the right time.

As a trader, you know that you need to make timely decisions when the strategy signals you to take one. When you have fear guiding you, the level of confidence drops, and you don't have the ability to execute the strategy the right way, at the right time. When a strategy fails, you lose trust in your abilities as well as strategy.

When you lose trust in many of the strategies, you end up with analysis paralysis, whereby you don't have the capacity to pull the trigger on any decision that you make. Making a move becomes a huge challenge.

When you cannot pull the trigger, all you can think about is staying away from the pain of losing, while you need to move towards gains.

No trader likes to lose, but it is a fact that even the best traders will make losses once in a while. The key is for them to make more profitable trades that allow them to stay in the game.

When you worry too much, you end up being distracted from your execution process, and instead, you focus on the results.

To reduce the fear in trading, you need to accept losses. The probability of losing or making a profit is 50/50, and you need to accept this fact and accept a trade, whether it is a sell or a buy signal.

The Fear of a Positive Trend Going Negative (and Vice Versa)

Many traders choose to go for quick profits and then leave the losses to run down. Many traders want to convince themselves that they have made some money for the day, so they tend to go for a quick profit so that they have the winning feeling.

So, what should you do instead? You need to stick with the trend. When you notice a trend is starting, it is good to stay with the trend until you have a signal that the trend is about to reverse. It is only then that you exit this position.

To understand this concept, you need to consider the history of the market. History is good at pointing out that times change, and trends can go either way. Remember that no one knows the exact time the trend will start or end; all you need to do is wait upon the signal.

The Fear of Missing Out

For every trade, you have people that doubt the capacity of the trade to go through. After you place the trade, you will be faced with many skeptics that will doubt the whole procedure and leave you wondering whether to exit the strategy or not.

This fear is also characterized by greed – because you aren't working on the premise of making a successful trade rather the fact that the security is rising without you having a piece of the pie.

This fear is usually based on information that there is a trend which you missed that you would have capitalized on.

This fear has a downside – you will forget about any potential risk associated with the trade and instead think that you have the capacity to make a profit because other people benefited from the action.

Fear of Being Wrong

Many traders put too much emphasis on being right that they forget that this is a business they should run the right way. They also forget that being successful is all about knowing the trend and how it affects their engagement.

When you follow the best timing strategy, you create many positive results over a certain time.

The uncanny desire to focus on always being right instead of focusing on making money is a great part of your ego, and to stay on the right path; you need to trade without your ego for once.

If you accommodate a perfectionist mentality when you get into trades, you will be after failure because you will experience a lot of losses as well. Perfectionists don't take losses the right way, and this translates into fear.

Ways to Overcome Fear in Trading

As you can see, it is obvious that fear can lead to losses. So, how can you avoid this fear and become successful?

- *Learn*

You need to find a way to get knowledge so that you have the basis for making decisions. When you know all there is to know about options, you know what to buy and when to sell, and learn which ones to watch. You are then more comfortable making the right decisions.

- Have Goals

What are your short term and long-term goals? Setting the right goals helps you to overcome fear. When you have goals, you have rules that dictate how you behave, even in times of fear. You also have a timeline for your journey.

- Envision the Bigger Picture

You always need to evaluate your choices at all times and see what you have gained or lost so far for taking some steps.

Understanding the mistakes, you made gives you guidance to make better decisions in the future.

- *Start Small*

Many traders that subscribe to fear have lost a lot before. They put a lot of funds on the line and ended up losing, which in turn made them fear to place other trades. Begin with small sums so that you don't risk too much to put fear in you. Once you get more confident, you can invest larger sums so that you enjoy more profit.

- *Use the Right Strategy*

Having the right trading strategy makes it easy to execute your trades successfully. Make sure you look at various options trading strategies so that you know which one is ideal for your situation and skills.

Many strategies can help you succeed, but others might leave you confused. If you have a strategy that doesn't give you the returns you desire, then adjust it to suit your needs over time. Refine it till you are comfortable with its performance.

- *Go Simple*

When you have a strategy that is simple and straightforward, you will be less likely to lose confidence along the way because you know what to expect.

Additionally, the easier the strategy, the faster it will be to spot any issues.

- *Don't Hesitate*

At times you have to jump into the fray even if you aren't so comfortable with the way it works. Once you begin taking steps, you will learn more about the trade.

However, you need always to be prepared when taking any trade. The more prepared you are, the easier it will be for you to run successful trades.

- *Don't Give Up*

Things might not always go as you expect them to do. Remember that mistakes are there to give you lessons that will make you a better trader. When you lose, take time to identify the mistake you made and then correct it, then try again.

Greed

This refers to a selfish desire to get more money than you need from a trade. When the desire to get more than you can usually make takes over your decision-making process, you are looking at failure.

Greed is seen to be more detrimental than fear. Yes, fear can make you lose trades, but the good thing is that you get to preserve your capital. On the other hand, greed places you in a situation where you spend your capital faster than you return it. It pushes you to act when you shouldn't be acting at all.

The Danger of Being Greedy

When you are greedy, you end up acting irrationally. Irrational trading behavior can be overtrading, overleveraging, holding onto trades for too long, or chasing different markets.

The more greed you have, the more foolish you act. If you reach a point at which greed takes over from common sense, then you are overdoing it.

When you are greedy, you also end up risking way much more than you can handle and you end up with a loss. You also have unrealistic expectations from the market, which makes it seem as if you are after just money and nothing else.

When you are greedy, you also start trading prematurely without any knowledge of the options trading market.

When you are too greedy, your judgment is clouded, and you won't think about any negative consequences that might result when you make certain decisions.

Many traders that were too greedy ended up giving up after making this mistake in the initial trading phase.

How to Overcome Greed

Like any other endeavors in trading, you need a lot of efforts to overcome greed. It might not be easy because we are talking about human emotions here, but it is possible.

First, you have to know that every call you make won't be the right one at all times. There are times when you won't make the right move, and you will end up losing money. At times you will miss the perfect strategy altogether, and you won't move a step ahead.

Secondly, you have to agree that the market is way bigger than you. When you do this, you will accept and make mistakes in the process.

Hope

Hope is what keeps a trading expectation alive when it has reached reversal. Hope is usually factored in the mind of a trader that has placed a huge amount on a trade. Many traders also go for hope when they wish to recoup past losses. These traders are always hopeful that the next trade will be the best, and they end up placing more than they should on the trade.

This type of emotion is dangerous because the market doesn't care at all about your hopes and will take your money.

Regret

This is the feeling of disappointment or sadness over a trade that has been done, especially when it has resulted in a loss.

Focusing too much on missing on trade makes the trader not to move forward. After you learn the lessons after such a loss, you need to understand the mistakes you made then move ahead.

When you decide to let regret to rule your thinking, you start chasing markets with the hopes that you will end up making money on a position by doubling the entrance price.

Things That Distinguish Winning and Losing Traders in Options Trading

Handling Analysis Paralysis

Traders usually start their journey getting the right knowledge. This knowledge comes in the form of books, coaches, and more. Once you have the information, the next step is to take it and use it in the market. The lucky ones will place various trades, and then things will go their way, while for others, the money will go down the drain.

Trading requires you to determine the right time to place a trade or exit one. The successful trader will know when to use a strategy, but the losing trader will end up placing trade after trade without any success at all.

Understanding the Nature of the Market

You need to understand that no market is constant – it changes with time. At times, the market will go along with your analysis, while at times; it might go the opposite direction.

Accept the Risk

No one wants to lose money on the markets. You need to come up with a strategy that allows you to know when to stop and reflect or tap out. At times you have to pull the plug regardless of how much you have invested in research and your expectations.

Know When to Take Profits

So, what determines the exit strategy? You need to know what point requires you to say this profit is enough for me. At times, it might be dictated by the changes in the trend or your rules of trading. Don't hold on to a trade for too long because it is always better to have some profit than wait and end up losing everything.

Understanding When you are Wrong

You need to remember that the options trading market is random, and you need to admit when you are wrong at times. This is because failure to admit will lead you to greed that might cloud your judgment.

When it comes to trading options, you have various traps that lead to fear or greed. Most of these traps come on expiration day; let us look at the various traps to avoid.

Traps to Avoid On Expiration Day

So, it is the day when the options are expiring, and this is the time you have to decide what action to take. If you are a seller, then you are anticipating this time because you hope to make some money out of the trade, while if you are a buyer, then you are dreading due to losses that might arise.

Either way, you need to be privy to some aspects of trading that will help you avoid any surprises.

Here are top traps that you need to know and avoid at this time.

1. Exercising the Long Option

You need to consider your options at expiration. At times, you can just close the options trade rather than buying the shares. Remember that when you exercise your options, you have to pay additional broker commissions that might not be ideal for you.

2. Options Vary From Country to Country

A huge percentage of the traders on the market use American style options to trade. However, other traders desire to trade the European options and this com with differences.

For European options, you can only exercise the option at the time of expiration, while American options give you the chance to exercise the option between the time you show interest till expiration.

For both options, you don't have to be stuck with the position till the expiry.

3. Holding Positions to the Last Minute

One of the hardest things to do is letting go of a position that you believe in. There are two scenarios under this – first, you have a losing trade that you just don't want to let go. On the other hand, you might have a position that is making you some money, but you think you have the chance to get more money before the options expire.

When it comes to trading, the final few days are the worst times to exit the trade because of the high risk that is associated with it. This means that the value of the option swings in any direction during these final days. Due to this, you can see your profits disappear in a few seconds!

The good thing is that you can decide to let the options go worthless and retain the premium that you collect at expiration.

4. Rolling an Option Position

Most investors are convinced that certain security if way better than another one. Many stock traders think that stock trading is much better than the options because they tend to expire.

If you are on a winning streak, don't hold out longer just to see the close; instead take the chance of closing the deal and making some money, however little. Using the rolling technique, you get to lock the profits in a position and then benefit from the profit. You can do this way early in the trading cycle as opposed to going after it when you need to close the trade.

Rolling gives you the ability to make some profits then use the original investment to pay for another option with a longer expiration period.

Chapter 7: Options Trading Strategies for Beginners

Whether you are a beginner, average trader, or experienced options trader, there are strategies you need to use to make options work for you. When it comes to options trading, you do not need to be a genius to make it.

Many traders invest in options without the necessary information. This is one mistake that results in self-doubt and lack of confidence in the trade. People who do this often give up as soon as they start. With the right strategies in place, you can easily make income, secure your capital, and make the volatile nature of options to work in your favor.

Trading strategies help you reduce risks and maximize profits. If you do not have any strategy to follow, the business can become difficult and costly. Options strategies vary from simple ones to sophisticated ones but have one thing in common – they are all based on put and call operations. The payoffs do vary greatly, and before you settle on a strategy, be sure to understand how it works, the expected gain as well as if there are any risks involved. As a beginner, do not get overwhelmed with a large number of strategies available since you only need a few basic ones to get started. You can add more of these to your trading plan as you master the game.

This book focuses on some of the most popular basic strategies in the industry. Generally, options trading strategies can be divided into three categories - conservative long-term strategies, semi-conservative or short-term, also known as aggressive strategies.

• Conservative strategies are accomplished on a long-term basis. These allow you to build your capital in a slow but steady process. The benefit of such strategies is that they reduce the risk of losing your capital.

• Semi-conservative strategies consist of four to six trades per day. These are more aggressive than conservative strategies and involve more risk as well.

- Aggressive strategies allow numerous trades each day. These often result in higher risks and small profits.

With this in mind, you are able to define the type of strategies you need. If you are a day trader, then aggressive strategies will suit you better. Now, let us look at some of the strategies you need to understand to get started in options trading.

Strategies Related to Calls

The process of buying and selling of calls is one of the easiest in the options trading field. It is actually one of the popular and frequently used ways to get into options trading. This is because it allows you to own stock, using very little capital. Buying calls also presents you with a higher profit potential than purchasing stock. Some of the strategies you can exploit when buying calls are listed below.

Covered Calls

Covered calls entail setting up call options against your own stock. This strategy is not only popular in options trading but in other financial institutes that deal with stock as well. In this strategy, you only sell options to protect your stock from downward price movement and also increase your returns. Most investors do this any time there is a possibility of good gains on their stock. In most cases, they sell out-of-the-money calls, and once the price goes high, they trade the stock for a profit.

One advantage of this strategy is that you get to keep your stock at expiration if it falls below the strike price. If the stock goes above the strike price, you will sell the stock shares to the buyer at the strike price. Most investors use this strategy to generate profit at limited risks while retaining their stock.

The downside of covered calls is that you need at least 100 shares of stock to make the calls. The strategy is thus not beneficial for traders who wish to start small. Traders are also allowed to sell only one call option against 100 stock shares. This is called a covered call because, in the event that the stock price goes high, the call will be covered by the position of your stock.

You can consider using this strategy to make a profit if you already have the required stock and do not expect its cost to go high in the near future.

Bull Call Spread

In this strategy, you purchase calls continuously and at specific strike prices then sell these calls at higher strike prices. Normally, the calls have the same expiration time and are related to the same underlying security. Investors use this strategy when there is an expected rise in the cost of the underlying asset, especially during high volatile periods. When used correctly, it reduces the trader's upside and lowers the premium spent as compared to buying covered calls.

The strategy lowers the cost of a call option and defines a limit within which the investor can generate income. Here is the procedure of applying the bull call spread strategy:

• Select an asset that has the potential to appreciate in days, weeks or months

• Purchase a call option at a strike price that is higher than the current market price. Specify the expiration date and make a payment for the premium.

• Sell a call option at a price that is higher than the strike price, but with the same expiration date as the initial call option. Do this simultaneously until the expiration time is reached.

By simultaneously selling call options, you will be able to receive a profit that will offset what you paid for the long or first call.

Since the strategy operates within limits, profits and losses are often constrained to certain amounts. This eliminates the possibility of losing all your stock to the trade. However, the disadvantage of this is that you cannot obtain any gain that is beyond the strike price of the sold call options.

Long Call

This strategy allows you to buy a call while expecting the prices to go beyond the strike price during expiration. One great advantage of this strategy is that if the prices go higher than the striking price, you can earn multiple times the initial premium since the trade has no upper limit. As the stock rises, the call keeps going higher. It is for this particular reason that long calls are common amongst traders who wish to make a profit from rising stock prices.

A disadvantage of this strategy is that if the expiration is reached and your stock is below the strike price, you may lose your entire premium. Therefore, use this strategy only when you are sure that the costs will keep rising until the option expires. If the stock rises only by a small percentage, you may lose part of the premium.

Long Call Butterfly Spread

This strategy combines the bull spread strategy and the bear spread strategy. These two strategies converge at the same strike price. Therefore, the long call butterfly strategy makes use of three strike prices. Just like the bull call spread, this strategy requires that you use call options derived from the same asset, and having the same expiration date.

Because the strategy allows you to sell two options at the same strike price, it is considered one of the low-price strategies that beginners can take advantage of. However, since it utilizes spreads of long and short calls, the chances of getting large profits are relatively slim. If the strike price is higher than the premium, the trade is considered to be bullish, and if it is lower than the premium, it is a bearish trade.

Short Call

In the short call strategy, you are required to sell your stock at a certain striking price assigned to the option. The main target of this strategy is for the call to expire worthlessly. The stock price must remain below the strike price for you to realize a profit. You risk losing your premium if the stock rises. Most traders only use this strategy when there is a high probability that the stock price will diminish. The more it rises, the more you lose money.

Related to this is the short call butterfly spread that involves selling one call option at low striking prices, buying two at-the-money call options, and then selling one out-of-the-money call option with a higher strike price. Profit is realized when the underlying stock's price rises over the higher striking price or goes below, the lower strike price during expiration.

Strategies Related to Puts

Buying of puts is one strategy you should use anytime you notice the market taking a direction that is against your call options. Traders buy puts whenever there is a possibility of the prices going down. Buying puts the opposite of buying calls. Here are some strategies related to the put option that may be of benefit.

Cash Secured Puts

This is the opposite of covered calls. This strategy requires you to sell puts against a liquid cash balance in your broker account. The only people who use this strategy are investors anticipating a decline in the stock price or those traders who wish to generate some profit from excess cash that is in their possession. Through selling puts against their cash, they are able to make some profit.

Generally, this strategy involves selling put options while saving enough cash on the side to purchase the underlying stock. It allows you to get stock options at discounted prices and sell them at a profit. The goal is to acquire the underlying stock at a price that is below the market price.

When the stock goes below the strike price, the put is assigned, and the trader allowed to buy the stock at the strike price. The process involves a lot of risks since the stock may decrease way below the strike price and this means that you may be required to purchase the shares at an amount that is above the current stock price. This comes as a loss to you, especially if the prices keep going down.

Married Put

This is where an investor buys stock and equivalent put options simultaneously. You can sell the put option at the strike price. Just like the covered call, each married put contract requires 100 shares. In this case, the trader is positive that the stock value will rise but uses a put option as insurance should the value go down.

The married put strategy is common in investors who have a vision of minimizing the downside risk of their stock. When an investor buys the shares and an option, he protects his stock from loss should a negative event occur and also makes some cash as the stock's value increases. However, if the stock does not go down, the investor loses the cash placed on the put option as a premium.

The married put has so many similarities with the covered call. It gets its name from combining or marrying a put option with the underlying stock. For every 100 shares, you are only allowed to buy one put option.

The maximum profit for this strategy is undefined. The more the stock appreciates, the higher the profits. One downside of this strategy lies in the cost of premiums. The put option increases in value as the stock value declines, and because of this, the trader loses the cost placed on the option. Such losses, however, cannot be compared to the value of the underlying stock which would have been saved in the process.

Long Put

Here, the trader purchases a put while expecting the prices to go below the strike price at expiration. It gives you the opportunity to multiply your initial investments in case the stock value falls at zero.

The long put has various similarities to the long call. The only difference is that you are expecting the prices to decline rather than go up. The upside of the long put is similar to that of the long call because the put option's value is capable of increasing in bounds. However, in this case, the stock should not go on the upside.

This strategy helps minimize the risk involved in shorting of stock. You must, however, note that if expiration is reached when the stock is above the strike price, the put option will be worthless and you will gain no profit.

The long-put strategy is ideal for use when you expect the stock price to fall before the expiration of the put option. The fall must be significant for you to return the premium paid; otherwise, you will end at a loss.

Short Put

Similar to the long put, the short put strategy is where you sell a put with the expectation that the price will rise above the strike price by the end of the trading period. In this strategy, you receive cash as a premium for selling a put. If the stock is below the strike price by expiration, you will be forced to purchase the underlying asset at the strike price.

The strategy is also known as the naked or uncovered put and gives an investor the right to purchase shares of an underlying stock when a put option buyer exercises the option.

For you to initiate a put option using this strategy, you have to be sure that the cost of an underlying asset will remain above the striking price. If the option expires worthless, you risk losing part of your initial investment. One downside of this strategy is that the profit is limited by the premium received, and there is a significant amount of risk involved. You should, therefore, use it only when they are positive that the stock will go up. You must also ensure that there is enough equity in your account to purchase the underlying stock should the put options work against your expectations.

Bear Put Spread

This is one of the best strategies for beginners since it involves short put spreads. The bear put spread can easily be applied to small and new trading accounts. It does not have any restrictions in terms of shares or premiums. It is also known as the short put spread and involves the selling of puts.

You can use this strategy when expecting the stock to remain at the same value or increase in price until the expiration date. If this happens, the option will expire worthlessly, and you will get your whole premium back.

To set up the bear put spread, start by selling a put option, then purchase another put option with a lower strike price than the one you sold. The option you buy should have the same value and expiration date as the one you sold. This makes your sold put more expensive than the one you bought, translating into some profit.

Unlike the long call, which returns multiple times of the investment, the short put spread can only give you a maximum return that is equal to your initial premium. This amount will be determined by the direction of the market. If the stock remains at the same level or goes beyond the strike price, you will get your premium back. If the stock decreases below the strike price, you will be forced to purchase the underlying stock at the strike price, and this result in loss.

Investors use this vertical spread strategy to make a profit from selling premiums to other investors who have bet against the stock prices going up. Because put sellers often have a certain number of shares to their name, they cannot get stuck when it comes to paying out on losses. In case you need to use this strategy, you must be careful that you do not sell your puts without first understanding the market. This is because stock prices may fall and claim all your premiums.

Other strategies combine put and call options to maximize profits. Some of them include the following.

Protective Collar

The protective collar strategy comprises of an out-of-the-money put option and a call option that run concurrently. This strategy is not so common in beginners, but if you master it correctly, you can lock some good profits from it. The combination of call and put options allows you to have downside protection to your stock while enjoying potential profits on the upside. It is the same us running the covered call and protective put strategies at the same time.

Investors use this strategy as another option to stop orders since they have the right to choose when to exercise their options. You can implement this strategy with little or no cost since the premium you get from the short call can be used to cancel out the cost of the long put. The strategy is called a collar because it helps you limit both downside and upside risk.

Long Straddle

The long straddle allows you to buy a put and call option at the same strike price, stock value, and expiration date. It is used by traders who predict that the value of the stock may go beyond the normal range, yet they are unsure of the exact direction this will take. The result of this strategy is often an unlimited gain. The loss is often tied to the combined premiums of the two options that are the call and put.

Iron Condor

This strategy combines the bear call spread, and the bull put spread. It involves selling an out-of-the-money put and purchasing an out-of-the-money put at a lower strike price. You then sell an out-of-the-money call buy a call at higher strike prices. Al these options are initiated at the same expiration date and on the same stock value.

The iron condor strategy is mostly applied to low volatile stocks in order to earn a net premium from the options spread. The combination of put and call options makes this strategy non-directional, thus creating a possibility to make profits either on the upside or downside. You can apply it on short-term or long-term trades depending on the performance of the market. The higher the trading range, the higher the profits realized.

Most beginners are always eager to start trading that they forget to look for the appropriate knowledge and skills for success. These strategies give you an opportunity to maximize profits on your options trading account. It is essential that you take time and build a solid foundation that will increase your chances of succeeding in your trades. The idea is if you do not know what you are doing, you will definitely end up losing your money. With a good strategy, you can start making profits as soon as you start trading.

Chapter 8: An Example of a Trade

Trading options is a lot more beneficial and profitable than trading in stocks. Additionally, trading options is much easier than what many people consider them to be. Let us look at an example of a trade.

Example

Imagine GRANK is currently trending at $80, and from your analysis, you feel the price will move to $100 in a few weeks to come.

One of the ways to make money from this is to acquire 200 shares of the stock at $80 then when the price hits $100; you sell it off. The decision will cost you $8,000 today, and you will then make $10,000 when you sell it off in a few weeks. This translates into $2,000 profit and a 25 percent profit margin.

Here is a breakdown of the whole process:

Type of trade	price	Sales proceeds ($100)	Profit
100 shares @ $80	($8,000)	$10,000	$2,000
1 share 40 call at $3	($300)	$2,000	$1,700
20 share 40 calls at $2	($4,000)	$20,000	$16,000

The good thing about options trading is that you can make huge profits in such a short time. This is only true when you understand the price movement within that short amount of time.

Let us break down the trade so that you understand what is happening:

Buying one call option contract (100 shares) of Grank with a price of $80, which expires in 3 months.

Let us assume the option was priced for $3 per share. This will cost $300 per contract because each option contract represents

100 shares. So, a price option of $3 means that the contract is trading at $300.

Buying a call option on Grank gives you the ability to trade 100 shares at $80 per share within the specified period, as long as it is before the date of expiration.

If the option goes to $100, the cost of selling the option goes to $20 for each contract, which means the strike price will go for a minimum of $20, which translates into $2000 per contract. This means the option has an intrinsic value of $20.

What Happens When Grank doesn't go up to $100 staying at $90?

If the price of the option rises above $80 by any value by the expiry date, then the call options are still viable with the difference of the current price minus the buying price. For instance, if it goes to $90, you can still make a profit of $10 per option when you sell them.

The good thing is that you don't have to sell off the shares immediately. You can still wait for the value to increase. You can hold on until the option reaches the price you desire.

What if the Price Stays around $80?

Now, what if the market price doesn't rise as you expected and just lingers around the original price till the expiry date. This means the option stays at the same price and will expire without making you any money. No one will be willing to buy the options at a price of more than $80 in the market. Here, you only lose the fee that you put up for the option.

What if the Price Falls Below $80?

Well, if the price falls below $80, remember you don't have an obligation tying you down to buying the option at any price – you simply do nothing just sit back and let the time run its course. You only lose the money that you put up for the option.

Key Takeaway

Always know that when you acquire an order at a certain price, you need to have someone that is willing to sell the option. You can engage in the options trading market as a buyer or a seller.

You also need to remember that options give you the ability to purchase the stock at a given price and then sell it before the expiry date. The call option requires you to call the stock away from a seller, and the put option requires you to sell the stock to someone.

Chapter 9: Tips for Success

Options fall among the most flexible trading instruments on the financial market today. They allow traders to make money from the downside, upside, and sideways movement of the market. There has always been a myth that options trading is both risky and complicated. It is easy to see options as something difficult to trade in, but this is not true. Only that using options as a trading instrument involves several risks, just like any other instrument. Not everyone comes out successful. However, anyone with good basic information about options can successfully make it in the market.

Most successful traders have tips and tricks that they employ to ensure they make some good profit trading options. Here are some of them.

Understand Technical and Fundamental Analysis

Before you start trading, ensure that you carry out an analysis of the market. Technical analysis involves the study of how the price is expected to change. The idea behind this concept is that you can study historical patterns in price changes and determine how the price may change in the future.

Fundamental analysis, on the other hand, helps you to analyze social, economic, and political factors that may affect the demand and supply of the stock you wish to trade in. Supply and demand affect the price change and can be used to detect the direction of stock prices easily. In a nutshell, technical, and fundamental analysis of the market helps you to identify similar patterns around the price and make informed decisions on your options.

Have Enough Capital

The reason why most beginners do not make it in options trading is not having enough capital. Most people get excited at how easy options trading can be and think that they can make an instant profit from their little capital in a matter of days. However, before they realize it, a few trades have swallowed their capital. They are then left with nothing to trade on. To be on the safe side, start with a good amount of cash that can sustain you for a number of trades.

Get a Suitable Trading Style

What differentiates traders is their preferences, personalities, and trading styles. You need to understand the style that suits you best. For example, some traders prefer working at night, while others are more effective in day trading. Some of the traders will make several short sales during the day while others will factor in the issue of time and volatility just to gain a large profit over periods that may last between few days and a month.

Learn from your losses and use the information to make better trades in the future. You need a lot of time to practice on a trade before engaging in the real trade.

Back-test Your Trading Strategy

Back-testing is a very important aspect when it comes to developing a winning plan. It entails evaluating your existing strategy and style against the market history to see how best you will perform. Although past performance does not necessarily determine future success, doing this will give you a rough picture of how your strategy and style may perform at different times and setups. In case you are unable to do this by yourself, you may engage a software company or Forex broker to do the back-testing for you.

One advantage of back-testing is that it helps you identify areas within your strategy that need to be improved. For the process to be accurate, you need to consider a few factors, which include:

• *Ensure the time period is accurate*. It is recommended that you test a strategy over long periods of time than short ones. This is because long periods often produce good results.

• *Stick to one sector*. If your strategy is confined on options trading, then your back-test should only focus on options trading.

• *Do not use results to make conclusive decisions*. In most cases, past performances may not necessarily reflect what happens in the future. As much as back-testing may depict your strategy as an excellent one, it is good to leave room for possible failure or underperformance of the strategy

Create a Risk Management Plan

When it comes to options trading, do not invest any money that you are cannot afford to lose. Before sealing a contract, think about the worst-case scenario in terms of what you may lose from the transaction and if you will be able to endure the loss. Beginners always have a problem getting over a loss. To help you remain on the safe side, do not put large percentages of your capital in a single trade. Always split your capital into bits, spare some money in an interest generating account, then use the rest for trading. This ensures that you do not lose all your capital in options trading.

Having a plan is vital for your success. You need to have it in place before you start trading. Remember, options are high-risk tools, and it is important to have strategies in place that can help you minimize the risks involved with each trade. Use your money wisely. Diversify the stocks you trade in to reduce the potential of losing all your capital. Most of the expert traders only seal a contract when there are low risk and high profits.

Be Patient and Disciplined

To succeed in options trading, you must develop a high sense of discipline. Carry out extensive research and set the right goals. Stick to these goals and have them in mind as you seize trading opportunities. Be careful that you do not follow the crowd and don't believe in some facts and opinions before doing some research. In other words, have a strategy that is independent of external influences. This does not mean that you ignore forums that provide you with useful information about options trading and the financial market at large. Just be sure to study the trends, learn from the market, and make useful trades based on your findings.

Patience will help you get the right opportunity to make a profit. Expert traders can stay idle for days, just watching the market and waiting for a good time to make or close a sale. Impatient traders will always complain of less profit or huge losses. Wait for the odds to work in your favor and focus on the bigger picture.

Patience and discipline will help you stick to your capital and risk management plans. These attributes also assist you to avoid trades you are not successful in.

Understand the Market Cycle

The options trading market keeps changing every time. You need to remain updated on the market trends and make the necessary adjustments to your plan accordingly. Through constant learning, you will be able to learn new strategies and identify better trading opportunities that another traders bypass.

Understand when to trade and when to exit. Know when the market is taking an uptrend or declining. Follow and interpret Forex news to understand what to expect in the future and where the industry is heading.

Keep Records

Having a record of your past trades can help you determine when to make a call or put option successfully. Some of the successful traders keep records of all their transactions. Analyzing these records continuously can help you identify vital patterns in the options you are trading in. It can also help improve your odds in the trade.

As you study the records, be sure to maintain some level of flexibility depending on your performance on each market. Learn how to exit a market that is not working in your favor. You must also accept any losses incurred since this forms part of every learning process. Options trading always deals with numbers so you must be good at making useful calculations.

Succeeding on Calls and Puts

As you may understand, there are several types of options trading, including call and put options. A call contract implies that the trader is expecting the price to go high and wants to make a profit from this increase. A put contract, on the other hand, means that the price is expected to decline, and a trader can realize a profit from this decline.

As you trade, you must be able to tell the direction of the stock to benefit from the call and put options easily. Beginners are always advised only to buy contracts to avoid the risk of using all the money set for the contract. Being a seller of an options contract puts you at a high risk of loss. Although your goal is to ensure that the option expires without you losing anything, you will need to part with an unlimited amount of stock if the prices go down. This leaves you with big liabilities.

Additionally, you must understand the difference between purchasing an option 'in the money' as opposed to doing this 'out of the money.' Purchasing an option in the money means that there is a value charged to your account in the options contract. This amount will be deducted from your account together with the contract price. Out of the money trading, on the other hand, is cheaper, but there has to be a change in the stock price before reaching the strike price for an option's value to be improved.

Mistakes to Avoid When Trading Options

At every level of options trading, there are mistakes that people do over and over again. However, these mistakes must be avoided in order to realize a profit from the trade. Some of the common mistakes you should avoid are:

Not Defining an Exit Strategy

Just like in stocks trading, you must be able to control your emotions when trading options. Once you have a trading plan, stick to it, and do not be quick to exit no matter how bad things become. To help you achieve this, define your upside and downside exit points in good time. You also need to define the timeframe for your exit, although the trade gives you an opportunity to get out of a call or put option before it expires.

Attempting to Recover Past Losses

A trade can move against you and make you lose money. Most traders have been there. Sometimes you may put your capital on options, and the outcome is not exactly what you expected. In such a scenario, most traders tend to double up their options strategy to see if they can recover the loss. Doubling may lower your potential for loss in a given trade, but it is surrounded by a lot of risks.

In most cases, it does not work. Most traders who try out this technique end up losing a lot more. Once a loss occurs, it is wise to close the trade and start a different trade to see if you can recover your money.

Trading in Illiquid Options

Liquidity in options trading refers to having active sellers and buyers on the market all the time. This is what drives competition. It also affects ask and bid prices for options and stocks. The stock market is often more liquid than the options market because stock traders focus on one commodity, while options traders often have several contracts to select from. An option quote always has the bid price and the asking price indicated on it. These prices do not indicate the actual value of the option. Illiquidity in options trading may result from illiquid stock. It is therefore important to trade options that are derived from a highly liquid stock.

Redeeming Short Strategies Too Late

Always ensure that you buy back your short strategies in good time. It is important not to assume that a trade will go your way the entire time. This is because trade can change performance in a matter of seconds. In case a short option gets out of the money, and you are able to redeem it then do so before you lose more money in the transaction. One rule of thumb that most traders use is that if you are able to keep 80% of your gain from a sale, then you should buy it back as soon as you can.

Do not allow yourself to learn the lessons the hard way. It is not always wise to attempt a trade while you already know the kind of risks involved. Focus on your trading plan and commit to these tips to succeed in your trade.

Chapter 10: Conclusion

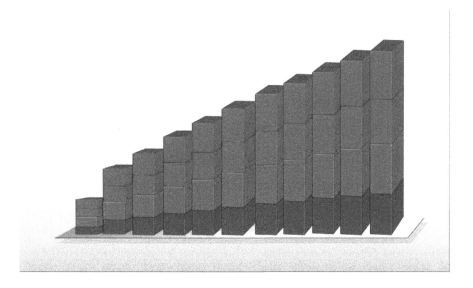

Options trading is such a unique yet valuable way of making money in the stock market. While there are some risks involved in the trade, these are normally limited, giving you a chance to make some good money from the trade. Adequate market research and knowing when to make a move will help you succeed in options trading. Brokers can also assist too since they can help you trade before you master the business.

After reading this book, you must have figured out how easy options trading is. With the information covered here plus your desire to make it in options trading, you have no option but to excel in the business. You are now better prepared to trade options using technical analysis, fundamental analysis, and other procedures. You are also ready to take opportunities as they come and have a sense of what each trade entails, from a technical view.

Trading in options is a process. The more prepared you are, the better the experience. Of course, the starting point lies in to understand what options trading is. Options are an alternative strategy for Forex investors who do not wish to trade in underlying securities. The basics involve understanding how to purchase and sell calls and puts. This is what constitutes an options contract. Let us recap a few points from this:

• An option refers to a contract that gives a buyer the authority to buy or sell an asset at a certain price within a certain period.

• Options do not represent the real value of an asset or underlying security. An option in itself is a derivative of an asset or security

• Calls give you the right to purchase an asset while puts allow you to sell an asset.

• The options market has four participants. These are the buyer of a call, the buyer of a put, the seller of a call and the seller of a put.

• The cost of an option is referred to as the premium.

• Long-term options are also known as leaps

With basic information at hand, you are now ready to attempt your first trade. How you embrace the strategies outlined in chapter 7 above determines how far you can go in options trading, especially if you are a beginner. The power of options lies in their versatility. However, this versatility comes with a cost. If not handled carefully, the trade becomes riskier than stock. That is why you will come across many disclaimers advising you to only engage in options trading using risk capital. This book plays a vital role in helping you appreciate the principle of decaying time and how it applies to options trading. Without understanding how this principle works, any trade that you carry out will be surrounded by diverse risks and uncertainties.

By now, you understand that there are a good number of tools and platforms that you can use to trade options. Since the cost of options keeps fluctuating from the start date to the maturity date, you need a platform that best suits your trading and training needs. Bear in mind that each platform has its strengths and weaknesses; therefore, you may not find one that is 100 percent effective. A good platform is one that gives you the ability to tailor your experience. Such a platform can accommodate both novice and experienced traders. A sophisticated platform can negatively impact your proficiency since you will spend a considerable amount of time trying to understand the advanced tools and features on the platform.

Having the right instrument will ensure that you trade with confidence.

Of course, we could not end the discussion without mentioning financial leverage as a benefit of trading options. The leverage comes about when you are able to translate your little capital into huge gains. It arises from the fact that a percentage increase in the price of an option is relatively higher than the increase in the underlying asset. This means that the more you invest, the higher the financial leverage. With a good trading plan, you can use this concept to minimize trading risks and maximize your returns. A great advantage in options trading is that the options contract itself is already a leverage opportunity. It allows you to grow your starting capital easily. By now, you should be able to calculate the leverage of any given position using the delta value.

While you can succeed in options trading without carrying out any technical analysis, it may be difficult for you to determine the duration, direction, and range of movement within the market. Since options are always subject to decay, any slight change in the values is very important. Understanding technical analysis indicators such as the RSI, IMI, and MFI can go a long way to ensure that you manage volatility, minimize risks, and close your trades with a profit. As a trader, you must always choose an indicator that complements your trading strategy and style.

When it comes to options trading, patience and commitment are key. You must be able to control your emotions. Emotional trading is a risky affair. Treating options like any other business can help manage losses with ease. Making trades just because they seem good can lead you into trouble. Actually, the difference between good traders and average ones is that a good trader does not allow emotions to control him. When he loses, he understands that it is because he made a wrong move or choice and that it is not the system that is working against him. Good traders do not dive into unnecessary opportunities just because of feelings; they weight the options and make decisions based on what is in the trade for them. They also understand when to quit from trade even if some losses are incurred.

We also looked at some of the tips you need to employ to ensure that you succeed in most of your trades if not all. These are simple things such as collecting enough capital before you start trading, identifying a suitable trading style, and having a risk management plan. You also have known some of the mistakes most traders make when trading options and how you can avoid them.

With all this insight into the options market, you should be able to carry out a trade from start to finish, successfully. You must, however, note that the options business is not for every investor. It can get sophisticated and dangerous if you do not put the information outlined in this book into practice.

By now, it is clear to you whether this is an investment you want to try out or not. If you are into it, then you must decide the kind of trader you would want to be. You can either be a day trader, long term trader, or a short-term trader. As a day trader, you will have the advantage of making several trades that close quickly. This option is good for you if you are interested in making small profits. Otherwise, consider long-term trading that can span a period of over 30 days but with incredible profits.

Like stated earlier in the book, trading on options also involves choosing the underlying security that you would wish to connect your options to. This may be in the form of commodities, stock, or foreign currency. Each currency has its own characteristics, and the liquidity status also matters. Commodities are good but very volatile, currencies trade most of the time, but the prices are easily influenced by economic news items. Stocks experience a rapid change in prices overnight.

To many people, options are a complicated instrument to trade in. However, the more you learn about them, the simpler they become. With some experience, you realize that the instrument is one of the most flexible to trade in. Nonetheless, for options trading to go well, you also need to understand the basics of picking a stock, assessing market cycles and formulating investment strategies.

Since options are highly volatile, if you do not exercise caution, you may lose all your investment at one go. That is why you need specialized training such as this one before venturing into it. A good number of people that have succeeded in options trading began as stock traders. If you are already into stock trading, you will have easy time trading options due to the many similarities that exist between the two.

Lastly, it is important to note that the shorter the trading period, the higher the stress and risks involved. If you keep holding your trades through the night, you stand a high risk of losing all your capital and destroying your account. Other than this, we are glad that you have learned a new way of earning money from the financial market and understood all the traits and skills you need to make it in binary options trading. Note that theory is never effective without practice. So, in case you need to get started, it is best to identify a trading platform and put what you have learned into practice. Remember, the more you practice, the more confident you become.

Options Trading

Advanced Guide to Make Money Trading Options in 30 Days or Less! – Learn the Fundamentals and Profitable Strategies of Options Trading

By Mark Elder, Brian Douglas

Introduction

Thank you so much for purchasing the book *options trading: Advanced Guide to Make Money Trading Options in 30 Days or Less! – Learn the Fundamentals and Profitable Strategies of Options Trading*. In this book, we are going to be talking about how to optimize option trading for advanced users.

Keep in mind that there are many ways to go about options trading. However, this book will teach you how to implement Advanced Techniques, which will help you to see optimal results when it comes to option trading. In this book we're going to talk about many things, more specifically we will talk about Advanced Techniques with options trading and how to scale options trading to the point where you can make a lot of money. As we know, trading, in general, is a precarious task and should have optimal knowledge before you get into it. This book is not for beginners.

This it is for people who are advanced to this topic and are looking to take it to the next level — keeping that in mind before you implement any of the techniques provided to you in this book. Make sure that you understand the basics of options trading before you start any of the advanced techniques if you try out the advanced techniques before you even know how to use basic techniques that you will not see any results, and you will lose a lot of money. This is just a fair warning for the beginners if you're advanced then you will see great benefits out of these techniques.

Chapter 1: Options Trading Advanced

In this chapter, we will talk about what an option trading is and also touch upon some stock trading as well. Even though this book is for advanced traders, we would like to touch upon the basics in this chapter. The reason why is because it is always good practice to go over the basics before we get into the topic at hand. Also, it is very important that you understand both stock trading and options trading before we get into the advanced topics. Overall in this chapter, we will talk about practical theory and examples which will help you to really understand what an option trading is and how you can yield amazing benefits.

Stock Investing

The market value of a share is that which results from the official price lists, if listed and may be different from the nominal value and the asset value (net equity divided by the number of shares), according to some variables. By simplifying, a solid company with good growth prospects will be associated with high potential and therefore a high value of the shares issued; on the other hand, a company with financial problems and with prospects of de-growth will be associated with a low value of its shares. Even the performance of the economy, politics, and speculation can influence the market value of an action.

How to Choose the Best Stocks

But which actions to choose? Upstream of this choice there must be a careful study of their tolerance to risk, also taking a cue from past behavior. Once you have decided how much to invest in shares, based on all the reasoning you have to do, you have to decide what to buy.

To this end many theories come in handy, the main ones are fundamental analysis and technical analysis. The fundamental theory tells when to buy, hold or sell a share, based on the prospects for growth over competitors, budget data, price, and dividend. However, the financial statements of companies do not always correspond to reality, since it is sufficient to insert an active or passive contingency to see the final result change. There are also the emotions of the market, so even under ideal conditions; it is possible that the value of action remains very low for a long time, perhaps falling below the purchase price.

Technical analysis, on the other hand, deals with the historical price trend, and purchase (or sales) decisions are made by forecasts. In reality, it is not so simple. What complicates things? The fact that even the market (companies, private investors, and institutional investors) probably uses the same tools, is observing and reacting, sometimes logically and sometimes in an illogical way.

Option Trading

This is also known as binary options trading. When you trade options, you do not have to purchase any assets. Instead, you simply have to predict if the price of an underlying asset will be higher or lower than its current price at the expiry date.

There are only two options to choose from: call and put. If you think that the price is going to increase, then you should choose a call; however, if you think that the price is going to decrease, then choose put. If you make the right prediction, then you can earn around 90% net profit. The rate usually depends on the offer of your broker. When you trade options, you will already know how much you can earn from trade since there is already a predetermined fixed payout. Moreover, if you think that investing in stocks where an increase of 25% in a year is already considered high, then you should think again. When you trade options, you can earn around 90% per trade. What's more, is that you can earn this quickly. When you trade options, you can choose from different timeframes. A trade can last for days, even weeks. But there is also what is known as speed options where the trade can be as fast as five minutes. In fact, there is also a one-minute trading time frame.

You need to be careful with options trading. Although it is a good way to earn lots of money quickly, it can also cause you to lose your money just as fast. If you make the wrong choice, then you will lose your whole wager. As you can see, options trading is as close as you can get to casino gambling. However, do not consider this to be a gamble. Of course, this will depend on your approach. If you just rely on pure luck, then you are gambling. But, if you take the time and efforts to do your research and all necessary preparations, if you consider every wager as a decision, then you are trading and not just gambling. Take note that this book does not encourage gambling. In order to increase your chances of success, you have to study the different assets.

When you trade options, you should pick an asset that is being traded. Now, you should research and try to learn as much as you can about this asset. The more that you know and understand an asset, the more likely that you can predict its price movement. This is how you can increase your chances of making a profit. If you plan on becoming a successful options trader, then you should be ready to do diligent research and analysis.

There are different strategies that you can use when you trade options. It is important that you use a strategy to increase your rate of success. You should learn about fundamental analysis. It is referred to as the lifeblood of investment. When you use fundamental analysis, you will have to focus on the basics. This is why it is important because it looks into the foundation of things. Once you have an understanding of the fundamentals, then you can more easily speculate how assets will move in the market. When you use this strategy, you should study the news regarding the asset concerned, the economy, technological developments, and the market in general, and others. This strategy is probably one of the most demanding strategies out there that require you to exert time and efforts; however, it is also highly effective. In fact, expert traders consider this a must if you are serious about options trading. Here is an example of how you apply this strategy: Let us say that you trade options with US currency. If there is news that the employment rate in the US is falling down, and all other things being equal, then you know that the price of the US currency will also drop. Hence, you can choose the put option and probably make a nice profit.

If you are familiar with the saying, "Knowledge is power," then this is what this strategy is about. It is about gaining quality information so that you can make your analysis and come up with a wise trading decision. Although there is no amount of preparation that can guarantee a positive return, using the right strategy can significantly increase your chances of making a nice profit.

Another important strategy that you should learn is technical analysis. When people think about options trading, they often imagine someone who looks at and analyzes a graph or chart. This is what technical analysis looks like. If you are more of a visual person, then you will most probably like technical analysis. The idea behind this strategy that all the elements that can affect an asset have their final effect on its price. Therefore, by simply analyzing the price movements of an asset, you get to deal with all these elements at once. After all, whether you make a profit or not will depend on the price. Hence, it is only right that you focus on the price of an asset. When you use this strategy, then you need to learn to read patterns. However, take note that patterns come and go. This means that not every time that you look at a graph or chart there is always a pattern to be seen. A common mistake is to force yourself to see a pattern to the point that you get to create a pattern even though there is none.

You can try to combine fundamental analysis and technical analysis. Many expert traders achieve continuous success by sticking to these two strategies. Of course, there are many other strategies out there that you can use, and you can even create your own strategy.

If you are just starting out, then it is advised that you start out small. In fact, you should take advantage of a demo account. Most options brokers will provide you with a demo account. This will allow you to make trades in a real market environment without actually risking real money.

Just a word of caution: Although options trading seems simple and easy, it can cause you to lose money quickly if you are not careful with it. So, remember to always back up every trading decision with solid research and analysis.

Just like the previous method, this method will also be a bit "theoretical," so please read it a couple of time if you don't understand it fully the first time. Now, there are two types of options trading one is call options, and the other is put options. So, in this chapter, we will be going through the two options, we will discuss how they work. So, without further ado, let us get into it.

Call Options

To explain call options, we will be using an analogy. Let's say you work in the automotive industry. You know the ins and outs of it. You also know exactly how much a specific car is worth and if it will go up in price or not in future, now you get some insiders news that the 1996 corvettes will be going up in prices in 6 months from now. Just like anyone in the interest of making some profits you start looking for a 1996 corvette, and lo and behold you find the perfect example of one for sale

Now, it will cost you $20,000 to buy one, and you only have $5,000 to spare. But you do know that you will be getting a bonus in 6 months for $20,000 which will cover the cost of the car, but unfortunately, it will be too late by then as the prices will go up. So, what you do is this: offer the seller $5,000 as a down payment for the car. You will tell the seller that you will have the full amount of $20,000 in 6 months from now for the car until then you will take the car off the market, and in 6 months you will buy it for a fixed price of $20,000. If you can't fulfill the cost of the car in the six months' time, the seller keeps the vehicle and the $5,000 and if you do have the funds ready in 6 months you can buy the car for the fixed price of $20,000.

Let's now talk about how this would work in the stock trading market, for example, if a stock is trading at $10 and you think it will go up to $20, what you can do is buy $15 "call option" for $0.10. If your predictions where right and the stock did go up to $20, then you could buy the stock at $15 even if the stock is at $20 netting you a profit of $4.90. But like in the analogy above there is a time limit, so let us say the stock didn't go up until $20 by the time you had predicted it to go up then you are out $0.10 cents, and the seller keeps the $0.10.

Put Options

Now, we will be using the same analogy for the put option as we did for the call option. So, let us say you ended up buying the Corvette for $20,000, to keep yourself and the car safe you decide to buy insurance at $1,000 for a year's coverage. In case of an accident or theft, the insurance company will cover your losses. Let's just say a year goes by and nothing happens to your car. You are happy that nothing happened, and you bought the insurance for your peace of mind and the insurance company is satisfied that nothing happened to your car and they get to keep the $1,000.

In another example, let's say your car has been damaged and it will cost you $4,000 to fix the damages. You decide to use your insurance to cover your losses, and the insurance covers your losses as promised. In the final example, your car gets stolen. Now you are out $20,000! Don't worry. The coverage is more than happy to cover your loss of $20,000 as it happened within the year. You see, the insurance company doesn't mind paying out $4,000 or $20,000 for your damages when you only paid $1,000 as it is getting the $1,000 premium from multiple people. They would need to pay out $20,000 in that year, but they got $1,000 premium from 100 people, which means they made $80,000 profit in a year.

Now let's use put option in a trading scenario. So if a stock is floating around $15 per share and you have a feeling that it will drop down to $10. As a safety net, you could buy a $12.50 put option for $0.10. If the stock drops down to $10, you will still have the possibility of selling it at $12.50 even if the stock is at $10. Netting you a profit of $2.40, on the other hand, this would leave the person at a loss of $2.40 who sold you the "put option." Now if the stock never drops down to $10 in a certain amount of time and the "put" expires then the put buyer is out $0.10, and the seller keeps the $0.10 as profit.

It Is a Gamble

You are now well educated on options trading, and you know that it can be a gamble. Therefore, I would not recommend making this your sole income as the cash flow is unpredictable. Exercise this method on the side to make money.

How much money can you make?

Just like stocks, you cannot put a number. People have made millions of dollars from options trading, and some have lost millions of dollars on options trading so like I said there is no fixed rate of pay you will be getting but also there is no cap on how much you can make.

Now before you go and try out your luck in this, please remember to know what kind of risk you are putting yourself into. There is no guarantee that you will make money or lose money, it is a gamble. For you to make it less of a chance, find out everything about the stocks you will be buying, know if it will be going down or up in price and then make your call. Just remember to make this your side income stream rather than your sole income as it could lead you to lose some money if not all. So, remember, practice with smaller amounts of money and have the discipline to stop when you feel like you are going into deep.

Chapter 2: How to Start Trading

We have already spoken extensively about how to invest in the stock market and how this activity can generate very high profits. Precisely because of a large number of profits that can be obtained, many are those who aspire to become stock traders: but how do you learn to invest in the stock market?

The point is that the Exchange is not a game: every time someone uses the term "play in the stock market" is taking you on the wrong path, because it is not a game, it is about investment. The best way to learn how to invest in the stock exchange is to start investing with an intuitive and easy to use a broker. The best solution in my opinion? Definitely 24option. Among other things, those who register for free at 24option also get free excellent trading alerts with which to invest in the stock market is much easier.

Invest in Stock from Home

The first characteristic of the investment in the stock market that immediately jumps to the eye is that it is an investment that can be made directly from home. It is no longer necessary to go to the Bank to hand over the purchase orders to the employee on duty. With a little nostalgia, the old traders remember those bank branches that had become a bit of a meeting place for the oxen park, given a large number of traders who met and exchanged information and observations. On the one hand, it is a positive thing, since investing in the stock market through an Italian bank is the best way to get skinny off of commissions and especially to lose money, given the inadequacy of the tools offered.

The only positive aspect of these oxen park meetings was the possibility of transmitting the necessary experience to those who were starting to invest in the stock market. Learning to invest in the stock market using the comments and experiences of older people is something that is difficult to do if you work from home. To solve this problem, it is obviously possible to attend discussion forums and try to establish a dialogue with the most experienced users. There is also to say that it is advisable to always go very carefully on the forums because of not all the information that there are correct. Add however that investing in the stock exchange from home, using tools such as binary options or contracts for difference, is great more convenient than going to a bank branch physically.

What are the best platforms to invest in home exchange? There are a few platforms that are truly reliable and affordable. Among the best platforms to invest in the Stock Exchange we can report:

Plus500: safe and reliable, it is a truly professional platform. Plus500 is a difference trading (CFD) trading platform that allows you to invest in thousands of shares listed in all major world markets.

24option: a truly safe and reliable binary options broker, perfect for investing in the stock market.

Iq Option: one of the most innovative binary options brokers. It is very safe and reliable. Offers a free unlimited demo account in time and quantities. Iq Option is the only platform for trading on the stock market that allows you to start investing with just 10 euros.

How to Start Investing in the Stock Market

The first step to start investing in the stock market is to know what the stock exchange is. It might seem obvious, but it's not like that: many traders start stock trading without even knowing what it is. The Stock Exchange is the regulated financial market on which shares are exchanged, which represent securities owned by listed companies. Each share gives the right, as the case may be, to receive a dividend (a portion of the company profits that are redistributed) and to participate in the ordinary and extraordinary meetings of a company.

Usually, however, it is not advisable to invest in the stock market through the shares. The best way to start investing in the stock market is to focus on derivative contracts that have underlying shares. In this way you get the advantage of increasing earnings and, above all, earning both when stocks go down and when they go up, obviously making the right prediction.

How to Learn How to Play in the Stock Market

At this point, you may ask how to learn how to play the stock market? The title of this paragraph is a provocation because we know that we must not talk about gambling but about investing. In any case, how do you start? How do you learn? The best way to start is options. These derivative instruments, in fact, are very simple to use and understand. In fact, binary trading is very easy: if we choose as a stock listed on a World Exchange (one of the main ones, of course), we only have to indicate whether the price of the asset will be increased or decreased at the end of a period of time. It does not count the level of variation, only the sign counts: and this is perfect for learning because the aspiring trader can concentrate only on a few fundamental factors, leaving out all the details. It must be said that options trading can produce profits so high that many traders are choosing to trade options only, although they do not need a simplified approach.

How to Operate on the Stock Exchange

We have already seen that to operate on the stock exchange it is convenient to use derivative instruments, binary options are better to start with and, later, CFDs can also be adopted (contracts for difference). Another important choice to make to invest in the Stock Exchange, especially at the beginning, is to focus exclusively on the best stocks, i.e. those of large companies listed on the world's major stock exchanges.

Among other things, the major options brokers and CFDs provide access to all the big stocks but not too small listed companies, perhaps in secondary stock exchanges like the one in Milan. In fact, these titles are usually extremely dangerous, and the novice trader who should choose them would be at serious risk of losing money.

How Investments in the Stock Market Work

For completeness of information, I try to make a global overview of the functioning of investments on the Stock Exchange. In general, it is possible to invest in the stock market with the direct purchase of listed shares or with the purchase of derivatives. In general, for those who have the problem of how to start investing in the stock exchange, the recommended choice is that of derivatives, in particular, binary options. For those who want to buy the securities directly, the process is slightly more complex: you have to open an account for the custody of shares and on this deposit, you, unfortunately, pay a salty stamp. Moreover, this type of investment usually passes for Italian banks and involves high fees and poor service. Vice versa, for those who choose to invest in the stock market with binary options or CFDs, there are zero commissions and a service that really works very well.

Another way to invest in the stock exchange is made up of mutual funds. Investments of this type work through the purchase of a share of the fund. The managers then use the money obtained through the sale of shares to invest the stock exchanges. This is an indirect investment that delegates all responsibilities to fund managers. In some cases, good profits can be made, but it has often happened that investment funds, especially if managed by

Italian companies, have led to very strong losses. Moreover, the tax treatment of this type of investment is strongly penalizing.

Investment Strategies

It is much better to do it yourself, then. But when you work with options or CFDs on the stock exchange, you need to have investment strategies that work well. In general, we can say that there are very simple strategies that allow us to predict the market trend based on the direct observation of the graphs. It is also possible to predict the market trend also based on the news relating to the various listed companies. Finally, for those wishing to delegate to others the choice of strategy without incurring the costs of investment funds, it is always possible to subscribe to trading signals services: in practice it is another trader (or group of traders) that indicates by e-mail, SMS or integration with the trading platform, what is the right transaction to do at the right time.

How Much Can You Earn?

The questions of those who aim to invest in stocks always stand identically from the day the stock market is born, and I would like to respond to these in-depth. Example queries:

How much do you earn on the stock market?

How to start playing on the stock market?

How do you earn in the Forum Exchange?

How much can you earn by investing in the stock market?

I lost everything in the bag

The last one will seem strange, but it is one of the many searches that many users make. They are traders who lose their investment on the stock exchange, and we should try not to fall into the same mistakes studying the financial markets and investing with a non-high risk profile and a diversified portfolio.

There is no time, in fact, that an investor does not ask how much you earn by choosing to invest in the stock market. To this question, it has never been possible to assign a precise answer. Most professional traders, in fact, know perfectly well that the amount of gain that can be obtained on the stock exchange is also linked to subjective factors. It is these latter that really determine what is then called gain.

The return on an investment in the stock exchange is also linked to a series of elements circumscribed over time. Investing today in the stock market is certainly not the same thing as an investment that took place over 10 years ago. In fact, then, it was in full expansion. The Ftse Mib, remaining at the Italian stock exchange, had reached very high levels and the performance of the individual shares seemed to improve continuously.

That era is officially over for some time. Investing in the stock market today means charging a series of risks unthinkable up to 10 years ago. Not only. Entire sectors of the stock market, such as the banking sector, are subject to an erosion of the price that seems unstoppable. This is another element to take into consideration when trying to understand how much you can earn on the stock market. Compared to the past, investing today in the stock market means to be aware that there are securities whose relaunch still seems very far away.

All the factors listed belong to the determination of how much you earn with the stock exchange. It is a variable sum linked to contingencies. But there is a way to calculate when to invest in the stock exchange and when not? In other words, is it possible to determine a minimum sum above which the investment was successful?

The minimum gain that can be obtained on the stock exchange to be able to talk about a successful investment is the result of a kind of summation. By removing the field from possible misunderstandings, it is always important to highlight that the factors to be added do not concern the subjective sphere of the investor. Instead, these are purely objective elements. The first, and most important, concerns inflation. When choosing to buy stocks, it is hoped that, at the end of the investment, the increased capital will not be lost with the increase in the consumer price index. Now it is clear that, when starting to invest in the stock market, the inflation rate is not known but only reputable. During the investment, however, we have all the information available to quantify what would have been the natural increase in the amount invested in light of the trend of inflation.

This makes it possible to get an accurate picture of the change in the consumer price index year after year. Assuming that there are zero risk investments on the market (a postulate rather than a reality), investing in the stock market is worthwhile if the yield is higher than that obtainable with the risk-free security. To do this calculation, you can take into consideration the government bonds of a highly developed country. The yields of these bonds, clearly low, must then be compared with those of the investment on the stock exchange.

The interest rate that is paid by this risk-free security must, therefore, be added to the index relating to the trend in consumer prices. Thus we obtain a first data which, however, is still incomplete. To define what is the expected gain of the investment on the stock exchange, a third element must be added. At this point, one enters the field of subjectivity. The third variable is an additional margin that compensates for the risk invested by the investor. Quantifying this third element is not at all simple. Traders, however, are used to quantifying the risk run in a couple of percentage points.

The definitive summation to determine how much you earn by choosing to invest in the stock market can be summarized as follows: inflation + return on capital + additional margin. In all-around 11 percentage points.

The 11 percentage points of return obtainable by investing in the stock market are gross. It is, therefore, necessary to subtract all the items of expenditure, including taxes. Furthermore, this is a level that is supported by a normal trend in the consumer price index. It is obvious; on the other hand, that today with low inflation, that minimum level tends to fall further. The summation alone, however, provides a partial picture of how much money should be earned "at a minimum" on the stock exchange.

A very important factor is the duration of the investment. In this case, the rule is very clear: to obtain interesting returns, hold shares for very long periods. This happened over 10 years ago. In fact, at the time, economic growth seemed to be unlimited, and the trend in inflation was positive too. In those years, the same stock indices improved continuously. But that picture has failed today. Paradoxically, to be able to earn on the stock exchange, based on the model mentioned, it would take an even longer period of time than 10 years ago.

All the major analysts say that investing today in the stock market makes sense only if the shares can be maintained for 10 years. It takes time to succeed, so, year after year, to accrue an interesting return. But over time it also serves a lot of confidence in a restart.

The example of banking sector securities is just the tip of an iceberg of what is happening on the stock exchange. If you look at the prices of many stocks in recent years, you notice the total absence of lasting restart. It is true that this situation is taking root especially in recent years, but who says that the picture will improve in a few years? This is the real breaking point compared to the past.

Today the balance risks/opportunities hang, and not a little, on the first course. The factors to be taken into consideration are many starting from systemic risk. The stock market trend, in fact, has to deal with the macro framework of reference and it is pitiless. The global economic recovery, in fact, does not take off.

Going down to the domestic market, the underlying picture is even more deteriorated. For this reason alone, investing in Italian shares is already a less advantageous step than an investment in US equities. All reports of the International Monetary Fund do not leave much hope in this regard: the difficult situation is bound to last in the future. The overall risk is then increased as further elements of concern have been inserted into this framework. The examples, in this sense, are the Brexit but also the serious crisis of Italian banks.

Therefore, investing in long-term stocks remains a bet for strong hearts. The fact that the long-term risks have increased, however, does not mean that it is impossible to gain on the stock market today. There is a way to avoid being overwhelmed by these fears. The road is to focus on the short term. The means to travel this way is to rely on binary trading and Forex & CFD Trading.

Alongside the various factors that we have mentioned as elements of risk to be reckoned with by choosing to invest in the stock market today, there are also purely economic considerations that advise against the long term. That 11% that we have indicated as the minimum sum that can be earned, in fact, is gross. In that percentage, in fact, various expenses are charged that derive from being a shareholder.

Those who choose to buy shares are subject to a series of taxes and are obliged to respect a lot of duties. It is obvious that if this happens at a time of financial expansion, then it is not a problem. On the other hand, if it starts at a time of crisis, then it is a further factor that discourages the long term.

Investing today on the stock exchange means relying on binary trading and CFD trading. In fact, only these two financial instruments make it possible to obtain a profit that is not subject to the many risks of the long term. With binary options and Contracts for Difference, it is possible to bet on the progress of stock even for very short time intervals.

This is especially true in the case of binary options. Investing in the stock market with options trading means betting on what is the direction that our action will take even in the 60 seconds following the opening of the trade. It is obvious that if the mechanism of operation of binary options is this, then all the talk about the risks of long-term investment makes no sense.

An options trading, on the other hand, is a way to defend against the high uncertainty that is ultimately characterizing the markets.

These same considerations apply in the case of CFD trading. The latter very closely resembles the traditional purchase of shares. With CFD trading it is possible to buy instruments that are linked to the performance of specific actions. You earn and lose in relation to the trend of listing but with a substantial difference compared to the stock exchange.

In fact, when you buy Cfd, you do not charge any duty. Also, the expenses as a commission are certainly not like those of the shares. Earnings, on the other hand, can be immediate. In this case, too, short-term investments can be carried out.

But where can you trade online today? In recent years there has been a boom in authorized platforms. This talk covered both binary trading and CFD trading. The list below shows the best brokers to earn trading with the stock market. It is good to remember that the use of these instruments can lead to the loss of capital. For this reason, before betting on online trading, it is always better to practice on demo platforms. These allow simulating the trading activity without risking losses.

All the best trading platforms give this possibility that it is exercisable without time limits. By joining the practice on the trading platform also a study on technical analysis and fundamental analysis, it is possible to create a valid alternative to the investment on the stock exchange. How much you earn today with online trading is definitely higher than what you earn on the stock market. Testing with a demo account costs nothing. Today, however, the role of inflation has become secondary. The curve of consumer price trends leaves no room for misunderstanding. Inflation is increasing nowadays slowly, and indeed, the risk of deflation remains around the corner. This is why we need other elements to define what we earn today in the stock market.

Chapter 3: Platforms and Tools for Options Trading

If you are new to the world of trading, this is quite a bit of information to take in, but with an example of each in the coming chapters, you should be able to internalize the difference between these two options and know their usage. For now, keep in mind that the example with the car is not fundamentally different from how an option works; merely the underlying asset is different.

Getting Started Brokers:

As a starting trader, your broker will be very important to you. Not just because you will want one with the lowest cost per trade, but also because you want the best research tools available to you. I highly recommend that you start with options Review – this brokerage house has the lowest transaction cost per option bought or sold and will be extremely useful when making the most profit off of trading a small number of options. Later in this chapter, you will see that the amount that you invest in an option is a function of your total investment fund. Assuming that since you are at the beginner level and your total investment fund is not all that large, the brokerage fees can add up quite quickly, and so this is a great firm for starting off with small trades. For the best research tools available, you will want to go with Charles Schwab Review. This is a broker that you might never even want to trade through, but rather make an account, keep some money there, and use their tools for finding the most up to date prices/indexes for different options.

Their tools feature a number of neat applications, like predictions on what the cost of options will be a few months down the line based on assumptions that a trader inputs. This is not an account that you need to create right away, but is one that will almost certainly be useful to you in the future as you continue to trade.

Aside from these two brokerage houses, you will have lots of different choices for picking a broker. I recommend just dealing with these two to start, and even from these, you will probably want to avoid Charles Schwab as you find your way and make a few trades first. Other brokerage firms offer toolsets that are not as good as Schwab or offer a transaction fee per trade that will be more expensive than an option. Bid Price/Ask Price: In our basic examples that covered the simple strategies of calls and puts, we were working with some very basic rules. For the sake of simplicity and to explain the mechanics of options, I removed the cost per transaction for options. This means more than just removing the fees that a broker would collect, but also not having to worry about a key aspect of the options market – the bid price and ask price for options. You will be relying on a lot of different sources to decide what commodities to write or buy options for, and chief among them will be the different exchanges that sell options.

These are indexes that list the most frequently purchased options, giving lots of information about the volume of options being sold, how they are being written, and when most of them are expected to expire. The most key piece of information will be the bid and ask price for options. The asking price is what option sellers are trying to get for selling one contract. The bid price is what buyers are willing to pay for an option. We refer to the split between them as the spread of the option. This concept may sound complicated, but the premise is actually quite easy when taken with an example. Suppose that you were interested in purchasing a call option from McDonald's. Don't worry about the strike price, expiration date, or exercise price. All you need to know is that you want to buy a call and that you know the underlying commodity is McDonald's stock. You would refer to an index on your broker's website, or refer to an index from one of the major listing boards, such as the Chicago Board Options

Exchange. Here you would find a listing of bid prices, asking prices, and the spread between them. These are typically listed in a per-share metric, such that if you wanted to buy one option contract, you would typically be multiplying the ask or bid price by one hundred to get the real cost of the option. This is because options are sold and bought measuring against 100 shares for each options contract. In this case, with the McDonald's stock, the bid price is $4.90 and the asking price is $5.12. The spread, in this case, is then $0.22. What this means is that a buyer is willing to buy an option on McDonald's stock for $4.90 per share, while a seller is willing to sell an option for $5.12 per share. You will also get a listing of the volume of the number of contracts sold in the last time interval (ranges depending on how you sort the options).

The spread is useful because it tells you how much you would immediately lose per share if you bought an option on McDonald's and immediately turned around and sold it. In this case, you would be buying an option for $0.22 more than you would be selling the option, netting you the loss of that spread per share on buying the McDonald's option. There is a lot of useful information to be gleamed from the bid/ask price, as well as the spread for options contracts. First, it tells an options trader how the supply and demand of a particular option contract match each other so that if the spread is quite large, there is either more demand for an option or it is in limited supply. Two, it tells the options trader how much they could realistically write options for on a particular commodity. Three, and most important to both options traders and general investors, it shows the possible direction of a commodity in the near future.

If the spread is quite large on McDonald's and the volume of calls is quite low, this means that investors believe the stock is due for a reversal in the near future. The lack of options being sold signal that there is a discrepancy in the number of options being offered versus the number of options that actually exist. In simplest terms, you can think of these three metrics, bid, ask and spread, as a way of determining the supply and demand for options on a particular commodity. It will be one of the most useful indexes when determining what commodities to write or buy options for.

How you use the information is highly variable on the volume of options sold, whether it is a call or put and other information about how a company is doing. It is not the end of all tool for determining the direction that a commodity will move, but it is instead just one tool among many. Searching For Options: The intent of this book is to give a trader all of the information they need to make intelligent trades right away.

You are learning about key strategies that are used at every level of trading to make a profit in any type of market. With this intent, I am writing examples that feature the laymen terms for expiration dates, strike prices, etc. How you will actually search for options will be a bit different. For example, say that you want to find calls for Microsoft that expire on July 20, 2018. This is listed as C-MSFT Jul 20 The first letter refers to whether the option is a call or put, followed by the ticker name of the company, and then the month and two digits of the ending year. To find the specific date, March 12th, you would look through the index of all of the calls that are being sold for Microsoft that expire in March of 2018, and sort by date. This will grant you the ability to find the specific end date that you are looking for.

In searching for options, you will find that indexes list a lot of additional information in addition to the end date, call or put, etc.

The lists show metrics for the changes in the overall cost of the option. This is based on the spread of the option overall, with the major metrics showing different ways in which the spread has changed over time. This is highly variable based on where you are looking up an index, but most of the time they will have common information like the percentage change in spread and volume of options for this date being sold. It is very important that as you are searching for options, you are doing so knowing that there are thousands of options for each company listed every month. Part of the challenge of invoking any of the strategies in this book is a matter of getting good at finding an option that suits your needs. Listing an option to be sold is simple enough, but buying one that will profit you takes some time getting used to. It is for this reason that I highly suggest doing plenty of searching on the brokerage firm of your choice before you start making any purchases. It can be a bit confusing to read listings at first, but a few searches and you'll get the hang of it.

As a final note, nearly all options are listed in the cost of the option per share. For example, a call for Starbucks may be listed as $1.10. The true cost of this option is $110 because the option must be purchased in increments of 100 shares. Also, since you may not be buying the option from the same trader, the call on the second hundred shares is likely to be a different price. It means that looking at the simple value of price per share cannot just be extrapolated to 200 or 1000 shares. You have to figure that the prices are highly flexible, and will not remain the same as you increase the number of calls or puts that you buy of any one company. Size of Investment Fund & Amount to invest: The size of your investment fund is going to vary depending on how much you want to put at stake for your options trading future. I make the recommendation that you do not start with an amount of less than $2,000. Any amount more than this is great, but this is really the absolute minimum that you will need to get started.

An ideal amount is closer to 4k or 5k. At these sums, your investment in each option can be quite sizeable, with good returns on trades that work well to your favor. It is key that for each trade you make you risk no more than ten percent of your total investment fund. This is the upper limit of how much you will want to spend on a single option. You should never be spending more than this percentage on a single option because if a trade goes poorly, it limits your ability to spread out risk in the future. Starting at $2,000, this means that each trade you make should be limited to $200. You will find that there are not that many trades that you can conduct with that much money. You will be able to buy a single option, instead of multiples. Also, the brokerage fees will play a more significant role as the percentage that they take from commissions will matter more. Most importantly, it limits the expiration date for your trades. Keep in mind that it will be, in most cases, a month before you can really determine if a trade has been beneficial to you. This means that you must assume that the trade is in limbo, and cannot count profit until the option is made liquid. In your first month of trading therefore, you can expect to make a maximum of around six trades with a $2,000 investment fund. This gives you time to learn from your mistakes, learn your style, and figure out how you can improve your trading game. In regards to determining the amount to invest, remember that writing an option contract will net you some amount of money upfront, but that you must calculate what your potential risk is for each contract that you write. As you progress to the next few chapters and start looking at more advanced strategies, you will want to focus on covered calls and puts, as well as plain straddles and strangles. These are strategies that tell you exactly how much money is at risk in each one of your transactions. If you start writing options for stock that you do not own, the covered aspect of this strategy, you are exposing yourself to a lot of risk for each individual trade. The money that you make in the immediate after writing an option is money that needs to be thought of as still at risk, and not something that you can bank; this is all in addition to knowing what your total exposure to risk for each trade that you make. If calculating your risk based on writing contracts seems difficult right now, that's fine; you will fully understand how to make these calculations when you are done reading the explanations for strategies in the following chapters.

Chapter 4: Financial Leverage from Experts

While it should come as no surprise that you are going to need to gather as much data as possible in order to make the best trades, regardless of what market you are working in; it is important to keep in mind that if you don't use it in the right way then it is all for naught. There are two ways to get the most out of any of the data that you gather, the first is via technical analysis and the second is via fundamental analysis. As a general rule, you will likely find it helpful to start off with fundamental analysis before moving on to technical analysis as the need arises. To understand the difference between the two you may find it helpful to think about technical analysis as analyzing charts while fundamental analysis looks at specific factors based on the underlying asset for the market that you are working in. The core tenant of fundamental analysis is that there are related details out there that can tell the whole story when it comes to the market in question while technical analysis believes that the only details that are required are those that relate to the price at the moment. As such, fundamental analysis is typically considered easier to master as it all relates to concepts less expressly related to understanding market movement exclusively. Meanwhile, technical analysis is typically faster because key fundamental analysis data often is only made publicly available on a strict, and limited, schedule, sometimes only a few times a year meaning the availability for updating specific data is rather limited.

Fundamental Analysis Rules

The best time to use fundamental analysis is when you are looking to gain a broad idea of the state of the market as it stands and how that relates to the state of things in the near future when it comes time to actually trading successfully. Regardless of what market you are considering, the end goals are the same, find the most effective trade for the time period that you are targeting. Establish a baseline: In order to begin analyzing the fundamentals, the first thing that you will need to do is to create a baseline regarding the company's overall performance. In order to generate the most useful results possible, the first thing that you are going to need to do is to gather data both regarding the company in question as well as the related industry as a whole. When gathering macro data, it is important to keep in mind that no market is going to operate in a vacuum which means the reasons behind specific market movement can be much more far-reaching than they first appear. Fundamental analysis works because of the stock market's propensity for patterns which means if you trace a specific market moved back to the source you will have a better idea of what to keep an eye on in the future.

Furthermore, all industries go through several different phases where their penny stocks are going to be worth more or less overall based on general popularity. If the industry is producing many popular penny stocks, then overall volatility will be down while at the same time liquidity will be at an overall high. Consider worldwide issues: Once you have a general grasp on the current phase you are dealing with, the next thing you will want to consider is anything that is going on in the wider world that will after the type of businesses you tend to favor in your penny stocks. Not being prepared for major paradigm shifts, especially in penny stocks where new companies come and go so quickly, means that you can easily miss out on massive profits and should be avoided at all costs. To ensure you are not blindsided by news you could have seen coming, it is important to look beyond the obvious issues that are consuming the 24-hour news cycle and dig deeper into the comings and goings of the nations that are going to most directly affect your particular subsection of penny stocks. One important worldwide phenomenon that you will want to pay specific attention to is anything in the realm of technology as major paradigm shifts like the adoption of the smartphone, or the current move towards electric cars can create serious paradigm shifts.

Put it all together:

Once you have a clear idea of what the market should look like as well as what may be on the horizon, the next step is to put it all together to compare what has been and what might to what the current state of the market is. Not only will this give you a realistic idea of what other investors are going to do if certain events occur the way they have in the past, you will also be able to use these details in order to identify underlying assets that are currently on the cusp of generating the type of movement that you need if you want to utilize them via binary option trades. The best time to get on board with a new underlying asset is when it is nearing the end of the post-bust period or the end of a post-boom period depending on if you are going to place a call or a put. In these scenarios, you are going to have the greatest access to the freedom of the market and thus have access to the greatest overall allowable risk that you are going to find in any market. Remember, the amount of risk that you can successfully handle without an increase in the likelihood of failure is going to start decreasing as soon as the boom or bust phase begins in earnest so it is important to get in as quickly as possible if you hope to truly maximize your profits. Understand the relative strength of any given trade: When an underlying asset is experiencing a boom phase, the strength of its related fundamentals is going to be what determines the way that other investors are going to act when it comes to binary options trading. Keeping this in mind it then stands to reason that the earlier a given underlying asset is in a particular boom phase, the stronger the market surrounding it is going to be. Remember, when it comes to fundamental analysis what an underlying asset looks like at the moment isn't nearly as important as what it is likely to look like in the future and the best way to determine those details is by keeping an eye on the past.

Quantitative Fundamental Analysis

 The sheer volume of data and a large number of varying numbers found in the average company's financial statements can easily be intimidating and bewildering for conscientious investors who are digging into them for the first time. Once you get the hang of them, however, you will quickly find that they are a goldmine of information when it comes to determining how likely a company is to continue producing reliable dividends in the future. At their most basic, a company's financial statements disclose the information relating to its financial performance over a set period of time. Unlike with qualitative concepts, financial statements provide cold, hard facts about a company that is rarely open for interpretation. Important statements Balance sheet: A balance sheet shows a detailed record of all of a company's equity, liabilities and assets for a given period of time. A balance sheet shows a balance to the financial structure of a company by dividing the company's equity by the combination of shareholders and liabilities in order to determine its current assets. In this case, assets represent the resources that the company is actively in control of at a specific point in time. It can include things like buildings, machinery, inventory, cash and more. It will also show the total value of any financing that has been used to generate those assets. Financing can come from either equity or liabilities. Liabilities include debt that must be paid back eventually while equity, in this case, measures the total amount of money that its owners have put into the business. This can include profits from previous years, which are known collectively as retained earnings.

Income statement:

While the balance sheet can be thought of as a snapshot of the fundamental economic aspects of the company, an income statement takes a closer look at the performance of the company exclusively for a given timeframe. There is no limit to the length of time an income statement considers, which means you could see them generated month to month, or even day to day; however, the most common type used by public companies are either annual or quarterly. Income statements provide information on profit, expenses, and revenues that resulted from the business that took place over a specific period of time. Cash flow statement: The cash flow statement frequently shows all of the cash outflow and inflow for the company over a given period of time. The cash flow statement often focuses on operating cash flow which is the cash that will be generated by day to day business operations. It will also include any cash that is available from investing which is often used as a means of investing in assets along with any cash that might have been generated by long-term asset sales or the sale of a secondary business that the company previously owned. Cash due to financing is another name for money that is paid off or received based on issuing or borrowing funds. The cash flow statements are quite important as it is often more difficult for businesses to manipulate it when compared to many other types of financial documents. While accountants can manipulate earnings with ease, it is much more difficult to fake having access to cash in the bank where there is none that really exists. This is why many savvy investors consider the cash flow statement the most reliable way to measure a specific company's performance. Finding the details: While tracking down all the disparate financial statements on the company's you are considering purchasing stock in can be cumbersome, the Securities and Exchange Commission (SEC) requires all publicly traded companies to submit regular filings outlining all of their financial activities including a variety of different financial statements. This also includes information such as managerial discussions, reports from auditors, deep dives into the operations and prospects of upcoming years and more. These types of details can all be found in the 10-K filing that each company is required to file every year, along with the 10-Q filing that they must send out once per quarter. Both types of documents can be found online, both at the corporate website for the company as well as on the SEC website. As the version that hits the corporate site doesn't need to be complete, it is best to visit SEC.gov and get to know the Electronic Data Gathering, Analysis, and Retrieval system (EDGAR) which automates the process of indexing, validating, collecting, forward and accepting submissions. As this system was designed in the mid-90s, however, it is important to dedicate some time to learning the process as it is more cumbersome than 20 years of user interface advancements have to lead you to expect. Qualitative Fundamental Analysis Qualitative factors are generally less tangible and include things like its name recognition, the patents it holds and the quality of its board members. Qualitative factors to consider include Business model: The first thing that you are going to want to do when you catch wind of a company that might be worth following up on is to check out its business model which is more or less a generalization of how it makes its money. You can typically find these sorts of details on the company website or in its 10-K filing. Competitive advantage: It is also important to consider the various competitive advantages that the company you have your eye on might have over its competition. Companies that are going to be successful in the long-term are always going to have an advantage over their competition in one of two ways. They can either have better operational effectiveness or improved strategic positioning. Operational effectiveness is the name given to doing the same things as the competition but in a more efficient and effective way. Strategic positioning occurs when a company gains an edge by doing things that nobody else is doing. Changes to the company: In order to properly narrow down your search, you will typically find the most reliable results when it comes to companies that have recently seen major changes to their corporate structure as it is these types of changes that are likely to ultimately precede events that are more likely to see the company jump to the next level. The specifics of what happened in this instance are nearly as important as the fact that statistically speaking, 95 percent of companies that experience this type of growth started with a significant change to the status quo.

Chapter 5: The Technical Analysis

In this chapter, we are going to be talking about technical analysis and fundamental analysis. It is essential that you understand these two concepts, as they will help you tremendously with the growth of your Option trading endeavors. Both of these techniques work very well when it comes to helping you make more profits out of your trading endeavors. Nonetheless, they both have their places. That being said, we will talk about technical analysis and explain to you what it is and the same thing with the fundamental analysis. And then we will help you understand which method works better for what, once you've been able to understand this you will be in a much better position in terms of making more money with Options Trading.

Technical Analysis

To put with technical analysis is, it is a way Option Traders finds a framework to study the price movement. The simple theory behind this method is that a person will look at the previous prices and the changes, hence determine the current trading conditions and the potential price movement. The only problem with this method would be that it is theoretical meaning that all technical analysis is that it is reflected in the price. The price reflects the information which is out there, and the price action is all you would need to make a trade. The technical analysis banks on history and the trends, and the Traders will keep an eye on the past, and they will keep an eye on the future as well and based on that they will decide if they want to trade or not. More importantly, the people who are going to be trading using the technical analysis will use history to determine whether they're going to make the trade or not. Essentially the way to check out technical analysis would be to look up the trading price of a particular stock in five years. This is what many Option Traders used to determine the history and the future of the stock, and whether or not they should trade using technical analysis. There are many charts you can look up online to figure out how technical analysis takes place. However, we have given you a brief explanation of what technical analysis is.

When using technical analysis, they also look at the trends that took place in the past. Most of the time, the stock fluctuates simply because of the trends that took place at that time, keeping that in mind, the Traders will look at the future and see if the trends will retake the place. If so, then they will most definitely trade or not trade depending on that's going to benefit them or not. Even though many people would consider technical analysis very "textbook," it is still very subjective. The reason why it is very personal is it because people interpret things differently. Some might think that the past will help the stock, whereas some might think it won't. Which is why technical analysis is both textbook and subjective at the same time. The reason why it is textbook is that you have to do a lot of research before you pull the trigger, and it is subjective because the final decision it's going to be based on how you feel about the trade. Many people say that technical analysis as more of a short-term thing; however, some still believe the technical report can be used in the long-term. In our opinion, we think that technical analysis short. The reason why we think technical analysis is short-term is that we are mainly basing our assumptions based on the past and the trends that took place.

Keeping that in mind, the capital gains you might see from technical analysis might be short-term. Meaning that the tray that you will make will not keep going in the long-term and will be a quick gain for you. Keeping that in mind, technical analysis is a great tool to use for people who are looking to make more money from Options Trading rather quickly, however, make sure that you do research properly on the stock before you make a trade on it. Many people make a trade on it by looking at the 5-year chart. However, it's much deeper than that you need to make sure that the trends that took place during those five years are going to retake the place. If not, then it will be entirely subjective for you to make a trade or not. The great thing about technical analysis would be that if you do it correctly, you will have a better chance of seeing success from it, and it can build a ton of confidence in new traders. This will be a significant thing for newbies or could be a bad thing for them since you will become extremely confident and make a blunder.

Fundamental Analysis

Fundamental analysis is more realistic and feasible in the long term. The whole premise behind the fundamental analysis is that you look at the economy of the country and the trading system that's going on to determine whether it is a good trade or not.

More focusing on economics, that's why it helps you to figure out which dollar is going up or down and what is causing it.

One of the greatest things you can do when it comes to Options Trading is to understand why a dollar is dropping or going up. Once you're able to understand that, you will be in a much better position for gaining profits in your Option Trading endeavors. When using the fundamental analysis, you will be looking at the country's employment and unemployment rate also see how the training with different countries overall sing the country's economy before you decide on whether you should try it or not. Many successful Option Traders solely believe in fundamental analysis, as it is factual, unlike technical analysis. Even though technical analysis is accurate, it is not guaranteed like the theoretical analysis. Instead of looking at the trends, you will be looking at what is causing the highs and the lows. Not only that, based on the highs and lows, you will be able to determine the country's current and future economic outlook, whether it is good or not. One rule of thumb to look into with be how good the country is doing, the better the country is doing, the more foreign investors are going to take part in it. Once starting the piece in it, the dollar or the stock in that country will go up tremendously.

The idea behind fundamental analysis is that you need to look at the countries economically and you also need to look at. To make you understand, what fundamental analysis is it is mostly when you invest in a country is doing good in the economy, and not invest in a company when they're doing bad in the marketplace. Which makes sense since the economy dictates how high are low prices going to be per dollar. Most of the time, investors will invest the money as soon as they see the dollar going up. The reason why they will do that is that they know the dollar will keep climbing up since the economy is getting better. One of the great examples would be when the US dollar dropped in 2007 2008, and the Canadian dollar took up, at that point, a lot of investors are investing in Canadian dollars of the US dollar. After a very long time, the US dollar was dropping tremendously, whereas the Canadian dollar was more expensive than the

US dollar. This was one of the anomalies which took place back in the day. If you were to use technical analysis in this instance, then you will not get a lot of success out of this economy drop. Which is why fundamental analysis could work a lot better or most people in the long-term and in the short-term, which is why many top traders recommend you follow fundamental analysis instead of technical analysis to find out which dollar you're going to be investing in.

Which Method to Use and When?

Now we get into the part where we show you which method to use and when ideally what Options Trading you would like to dabble with technical analysis and fundamental analysis to see optimal success. However, you can do fundamental analysis and see progress, both long-term and short-term. In our opinion the best way to go about it would be to try out technical analysis in the short-term, the reason why we think the technical analysis, in short, would work very good for you is that it is something that you can't go wrong with if you do it properly. As we explained to you what technical analysis is, you can see why it is so good for someone to start with technical analysis and to see amazing results out of it. Another thing technical analysis can help you out with would be that it will help you to build up your confidence in the beginning. When you're starting Option Trading especially in the beginning, it is essential that you build up confidence and you make yourself believe that you can, make money from Options Trading.

This will help you to continue with your Options Trading journey and to learn more, more accurately help you to start investing your money the right way and to continue off becoming a full-time Option Trader. Once you have dabbled with technical analysis, you can start doing your more long-term trades with fundamental analysis. The only problem with fundamental analysis would be that there's a lot more research to be done, and if you're trying to make Options Trading a long-term income Source or a full-time income Source, then the chances are you should be doing your research before you make a trade. Keep in mind that, fundamental analysis will help you to keep going in the long-term and will yield you the best results possible. Even though technical analysis has a higher success rate, fundamental analysis will be a lot more long-term. Secondly, the more you do fundamental analysis, the easier it's going to get for you.

Keeping that in mind, the best method to go about Options Trading, in the beginning, would be to start with technical analysis make small trades, and make some money. This will help you to build up your confidence with Options Trading and therefore help you to keep going on. The second thing you should be doing is research on the fundamental analysis I'm slowly started dabbling with it until you are sure on which dollar or stock on investing based on your research. You will require some brainpower to really dabble with Options Trading using fundamental analysis. However, once you understand it and start dabbling with it, you will see the success they looking for with Options Trading. The final verdict would be to use both of them however used technical analysis, in the beginning, to really see some short-term benefits out of it and then eventually branch off to fundamental analysis and then dabbing our technical analysis trading there to see the small incremental games. When combined both you will be in a much better position to make a lot of money from Options Trading.

Chapter 6: Mindset Controlling Your Emotions like a Pro

We will talk about what you should be doing, to make sure that you are not failing in your endeavors to start your options trading journey without making it too hard on yourself. In this chapter will show you what you could be doing to make options trading your lifestyle and to not only help you to start your trading journey but to stay on track. These daily patterns will help you not to fail when trading, and we understand that you might fail a couple of times in anything you do, and it is understandable to do so. Nonetheless, this chapter will show you how to make sure you are consistent and not failing. Many successful people have followed these habits, to get optimal results in all of their aspects of life, whether it be job-related or anything else. Make sure you start implementing all of these habits after you are done reading this book as it will help you to make options trading much easier for you. The reason why this chapter might sound philosophical is that the only way you will see success with options trading is if you do it consistently. For you to do that, you need to change your current lifestyle by being more productive and disciplined. You have to remember, being successful in options trading is more of a lifestyle.

Plan Your Day Ahead

Planning your day ahead of time is crucial, not only does planning out your day help you be more prepared for your day moving forward, but it will also help you to become more aware of the things you shouldn't be doing, hence wasting your time.

Moreover planning your day will truly help you with making the most out of your time, that being said we will talk about two things 1.Benefits of planning out your day 2. How to go about planning out your day. So without further ado, let us dive into the benefits of planning out your day.

It will help you prioritize:

Yes, planning out your day will help you prioritize a lot of things in your day to day life. You can allow time limits to the things you want to work on the most to least, for example, if you're going to write your book and you are super serious about it. Then you need a specific time limit every day in which you work on a task wholeheartedly without any worries of other things until the time is up. Then you move on to the next job in line, so when you schedule out your whole day, and you give yourself time limits, then you can prioritize your entire day. The same thing goes for your trading, make sure you allocate time for trading, which will allow you to be more focused on your research, hence making you more successful.

Summarize your normal day:

Now, before we start getting into planning out your whole day ahead, you need to realize that to plan your entire day, you need to know precisely what you are doing that day. Which means you need to write down every single thing you do on a typical day and write down the time you start and end, it needs to be detailed in terms of how long does it take for your transportation to get to work, etc.

Now after you have figured out your whole day, you can decide how to prioritize your day moving on could be cutting out a task that you don't require or shortening your time for a job that doesn't need that much time. After you have your priorities for the day, you can add pleasurable tasks into your day like hanging out with your friends, etc.

Arrange your day:

It is crucial that you arrange your day correctly, so the best way to organize your day is to make sure you get all your essential stuff done earlier in the day when your mind is fresh. After that's done, you can have some time for yourself to relax and do whatever it is that you want. But make sure you get all the things that need to be done before you can move on to free time for yourself. Another thing that will help you is to set time limits on each task, and once you start setting time limits, you will be more likely to get the job done.

Remove all the fluff:

So, what I mean by that is remove all the things that are holding you back from achieving your goals. Make sure you remove all of the things that are holding you back from getting the things that you need to be doing. If you have time for the fluff, do it if not, then work on your priorities first. In conclusion, planning out your day will help you tremendously! Make sure you plan out your day every day to ensure successful and accomplished days.

Cut out negative people:

This task might be the hardest to do, but it is quite essential, see the people who you are around are the people who will create your personality. So if you are around negative people, you will develop adverse circumstances for yourself, so if you are around people who are not upbeat about life and find everything wrong and never see the good in anyone, you need to cut them out and be around people who are happy and ready for what life has to offer. Now I get it, some cynical people can be your family members, and you can't cut them out, the ideal thing to do is 1. Make them understand what they are doing wrong 2. Show them how they can change their life. And if they still want to remain the same, then keep your distance.

In conclusion, it is essential that you are in a grateful "vibe" as it will not only help you with your mental and physical health, but it will also help you attract better people and better circumstances. Don't forget to practice the three methods we discussed in this chapter for you to be in a grateful 'vibe" throughout the day and life! That being said I hope this chapter shed some light on the importance of being grateful and how it can make or ruin a living, and I hope you don't take this chapter lightly being grateful is the most critical thing you can do to turn your life around. So be thankful!

Now that we have covered the part of being grateful, and how it can help you with your day to day life and eating habits. Let us give you some concrete ideas on how to change the way you live your experience and to make it better.

Stop Multitasking

I think we are all guilty of this at a time, and if are multitasking right now, I need you to stop. Now multitasking could be a lot of things, and it could be as small as cooking and texting at the same time, or it could be as big as working on two projects at the same time. Studies are showing how multitasking can reduce your quality of work, which something you don't want to do if your goal is to get the best result out of the thing that you are doing. That being said, there are a lot more reasons as to why you shouldn't be multitasking, so without further ado, let's get into the primary reasons why multitasking can be harmful.

You're Not as Productive.

Believe it or not, you tend to be a lot less productive when you are multitasking. When you go from one project to another or anything else for that matter, you don't put all your effort into your work. You are always worried about the project that you will be moving into next. So moving back and forth from one project to another will affect your productivity if you want to get the most out of your work you need to be focused on one thing at a time and make sure you get it done to the best of your abilities. Plus you are more likely to make mistakes, which will not help you work at the best of your ability.

You Become Slower at Your Work.

When you are multitasking, chances are you will end up being slower at completing your projects. You would be in a better position if you were to focus on one project at a time instead of going back and forth, which of course helps you complete them faster. So the thing that enables you to be faster at your projects when you're not multitasking is the mindset, we often don't realize how much mindset comes into play. When you are going back and forth from one project to another, you are in a different mental state going into another project which takes time to build and break. So by the time you have managed to get into the mindset of project A you are already moving into project B, it is always best that you devote your time and energy one project at a time if you want it to doe did an at a faster pace.

Set Yourself a Goal (time, quality, etc.)

All in all, multitasking will do you no good. It will only make you slower at your work and make you less productive. Making sure you stop multitasking is essential, as it will only help you live a better life. One thing to remember from this chapter is to put all your energy at one thing at a time, and this will yield you a lot better projects or anything that you are working towards to be great. If you want to be more successful and live a better life, you need to make sure your projects are quality as I can't stress this point enough. You are probably reading this book because you want to get better at living your life or achieve goals which you haven't yet. One of the reasons why you are not living the life that you want or haven't reached your goal could be a lot of things but, one of the items could be the quality of your work which could be taking a hit because of your multitasking. So review yourself, and find out why you haven't achieved your goal and why you are not living the life that you want.

Then if you happen to stumble upon multitasking being the limiting factor or the quality of your work, I want you to stop multitasking and start working on one project at a time while giving it your full attention. What you will notice is that your work will have a higher quality and will be completed in a quicker amount of time following the steps listed above, which will change your life and help you achieve your life goals in a better more efficient way.

Now that we have talked about some action items in regards to making options trading more of a lifestyle by changing the way you set up your day. Let us talk about some of the lifestyle changes you need to make, in regards to making trading more easy for you.

Get More Sleep.

It is essential that you start getting your 8 hours of sleep. Many people don't know this but, even if your eating is perfect but you still aren't getting the sleep chances are you are not going to see the changes. Getting your 8 hours of sleep helps you a lot. When you get the right amount of deep sleep, you will see results such as better recovery and better mental health. It is essential that you get your full 8 hours of sleep if you don't, then your option trading endeavors might go to vain. Not only that, if you don't get enough sleep, the chances of you staying awake the next morning will drop down tremendously. You will be a lot more sleepy the days you don't get your full sleep. Keep that in mind moving on, and as always make sure to get your total 8 hours of sleep.

Physical Activity

It is very crucial for you to take part in physical activities, for a straightforward reason it will help you to assist your motivation to trade. The same thing as getting proper sleep, the role of you being physically active will give you a great balance of you being energized and motivated throughout the day. Many people don't know this, but being physically active can help you to stay more motivated. There have been many studies backing these claims up, that being said, let's talk about some of the benefits which might come along with you following a working out plan.

Regular Exercising Changes Your Brain

No, regular exercises do not change the way your brain is shaped by any means if that's what you're thinking. But what it will help with, is better memory and better-thinking skills. If you were to do your research, you will find that out for yourself, how big of a role regular exercising plays when it comes to brain functions.

Make sure you start implementing this physical activity, it will only help you get better at your trading skills and to see better results out of it. By now you can see the benefits of exercising, not only does regular exercising help you stay healthy physically, but it also enables you to optimize your mind and helps you with better brain function which will allow you to work for an extended period at any given task.

Improves your mood:

This is one of the most significant differences you will notice once you start working on your health is that your mood will stay elevated through the day! Which is a great thing to have as you will be able to get more things done and be more successful? See when you work out you release a chemical called dopamine, which is a feel-good hormone and of course working out will help you become less stressed.

Improves physical health:

Yes, this is one of the most salient points to bring up but let's discuss it anyway. Once you start to implement healthy habits to your day you will become more physically fit, which will not only give you more energy through the day, it will also help you keep up with things like your daily chores and not get tired so quickly.

You will see a difference in the quality of your life and your work ethic once you start to implement daily health habits and become more physically healthy.

Helps boost your immune system:

These ties into improved physical health, but working out will boost your immune system and lower your risk of diseases like diabetes, hypertension, etc. Once you have a boost in your immune system, you will be less likely to get even the common flu. I know of someone who hasn't gotten flu in fifteen years simply because he started to live a healthy life, now I am not saying that you will see the same results but staying healthy will definitely help you with boosting your immune system which will help you not get sick so often and enjoy some quality time with your family and get more stuff done.

Now that we have discussed how staying in shape can help you live a better life, we will now move on to the ways you can help yourself live a healthier life.

Start easy:

Now, if you have never worked out in your life, you need to realize that you won't be going hard at the gym as Arnold Schwarzenegger did in his hay days. So don't push yourself too much in the gym because you are not ready for it, and you might lose motivation. So if you are starting off getting in shape perhaps light jogs, some resistance training couple times a week to get the blood moving. But make sure you get up to the point where you are working out at least three hours a week to see some health benefits. Start once a week then twice, and so on.

After reading this chapter, many might be thinking that this is more of a self-help book than it is options trading. The truth is that we want you to understand how to live a better life by changing the habits that you are currently following. Doing option trading and making it a lifestyle is a lot more work than you think it is. For you to make it easy, you need to understand that you need to change your habits to be successful at option trading, which means you need to change the way you move the way you think and the way you perform. This chapter gives you a clear idea on how to start living a better life by changing up your habits, once you do change your practices you will notice that options trading as a whole will be straightforward for you.

The reason why it will be straightforward for you is that you will change the way you move and the change the way you live your life in general. Changing the way you live your life will not only help you get better results, but it will also help you to make options trading a lifestyle, many people confuse income source as not being a part of a lifestyle, and it is something that they're supporting to better their health. But the truth is that when they're working on trading, they don't realize that it needs to be a lifestyle for it to be a health benefit, if you want to be healthier then you need to make sure that you're taking care of your health 24/7 365 days a year.

Which means you need to make this a lifestyle, and for you to make this a lifestyle, we need to understand some self-help techniques to keep it sustained for a more extended period. Which is why this chapter is more self-help oriented, we wanted to make sure that this book is different than any other books that you've read when it comes to starting your options trading journey. The way we're going to be delivering it is by showing you how to change your lifestyle for the better instead of the worst. With that being said, I hope this chapter was helpful to you, and we will see you in the next chapter.

Chapter 7: Options Trading Strategies for Experts

While it can be easy to feel as though there is too much information out there regarding options trading to ever hope to keep it straight, there are several key strategies you will use on a regular basis that you can focus on at the start to make the entire process far more manageable. As long as you take the time to utilize them correctly, you will find that each of the strategies outlined below will dramatically improve your success rate while decreasing your overall risk at the same time.

Keep in mind that the strategies that you use aren't nearly as important as the fact that you choose strategies that suit your trading style and compliments the trading plan you are focused on using for the time being. Keep in mind that just because a strategy seems useful, doesn't mean it is going to be useful in your hands. Play name: Buy/write Who should run it: This strategy is suitable for everyone When to run it: This strategy is effective in a bearish market Details: Sometimes referred to as the covered call, this strategy works when the trader purchases shares of an underlying stock while at the same time generating a call that is equal to the entire number of underlying stock shares owned. This strategy is ideal for traders who have already invested in the stock market and are looking for a way to shore up what may be previously questionable choices as the options will ensure that you can generate a premium even if the other bets placed in the investment don't exactly pay off. This is an especially viable way to ensure long term investments remain viable as the option will guarantee a profitable price for the length of its existence. This makes the covered call strategy ideal for LEAPs, index future and funds whose purchase was facilitated via margin.

Play name: Married put Who should run it: This strategy is suitable for everyone When to run it: This strategy is effective in a bullish market Details: A married put is a great strategy if you have reason to take a bullish attitude towards the price of a given underlying asset while at the same time aiming to shore up any potential losses you might come across. To use this strategy properly, the first thing you will need to do is to purchase any amount of the underlying asset in question while tat the same time purchasing a put that covers the same amount. This will act as the price floor that will help you to prevent serious, unexpected losses in the case of a sudden price drop. While adding more money to a losing proposition is never the best choice, a married put can be used to shore up an existing investment that hasn't turned out as you hoped.

Regardless of the size of your portfolio, this is a useful strategy to mitigate the risk that can't be dealt with in any other way. While the married put will not be the best choice in any situation, if used in the right way, and with plenty of caution, it can be a reliable way to improve your successful trading percentage successfully. To ensure this always works out in your favor, you will never want to begin a new transaction without having a clear understanding of the risk you are working with beforehand. You will then be able to factor in additional costs more easily and compare the total cost to the amount of risk you are going mitigate as a result. After that, all that's left is going to be doing the math and choosing the option that makes the most fiscal sense at the moment. What's more, married puts also help to reduce the potential for risk when it comes to new options to exercise as it ensures you always have available shares waiting in the wings. Play name: Bull call spread who should run it: This strategy is suitable for everyone When to run it: This strategy is effective in a bullish market Details: To utilize the bull call spread successfully, you will want to start with a call option that is purchased at a strike price that is worth returning to in the future. You will also need to sell an equal number of calls at a strike price that is above the initial strike price yet still within a reasonable distance. Both of these calls will also need to include the same timeframe as well as the same underlying asset. This is an excellent strategy to use if you feel bullish on the strength of the asset in question or you have research that shows the price is likely to increase during your chosen timeframe. This strategy also goes by the name vertical credit spread thanks to its mismatched legs.

Those that sell close to the money result in a credit spread that includes a positive time value and a net credit. Debit spreads are created if a short option ends further away from the money than the point it started from. Regardless, you can consider this strategy a net buy. Play name: Bear put spread Who should run it: This strategy is suitable for everyone When to run it: This strategy is effective in a bearish market Details: Similar in practice to the bull call spread, the bear put spread is useful under different circumstances. To use it effectively, you will need to purchase a pair of put options that have different strike prices, own lower and one higher. You will then need to purchase an equal number with the same timeframe and the same underlying asset. This can be an especially useful strategy if you have a bearish opinion of the underlying asset in question as it will help to limit your losses if you judge the market incorrectly. It is still important to be cautious, however, as the profits that it will bring you are always going to be limited to the difference between the two puts you initially purchased, minus any relevant fees. The most profitable time to utilize this strategy is if you are already planning on short selling a specific underlying asset and a traditional put option won't provide you with the protection you need.

You will likely find them especially useful if you plan on speculating and also feel that prices are going to decrease. This will allow you to avoid employing additional capital while only waiting for the worst to happen. As such, you will be able to hope for the best and plan for the worst at the same time. Play name: Protective collar Who should run it: This strategy is suitable for everyone When to run it: This strategy is effective in a bullish or bearish market Details: The protective collar strategy can be executed by buying into a put option that is already out of the money. From there, you will then want to write a secondary call option that is based on the same underlying asset and is also out of the money. After that, you will then be able to create a secondary call option that is based on the same underlying asset that is also out of the money already. Thus, this strategy is useful if you are already committed to a long position on an underlying asset that has a history of strong gains. Using a protective collar properly then allows you to ensure that you can anticipate a steady level of Profit while also retaining control of the underlying asset if the positive trend does continue. Using a protective collar correctly is as easy as ensuring the contract for the put option you purchased was at a strike price that is more than likely enough to ensure you will hold onto most of the profits you banked throughout the process. After that, you will then be able to fund the collar strategy using the call option you previously created. This strategy is advantageous if you are looking to maintain your profits at all costs as it only requires a small additional fee. What's more, this is an excellent way to move funds about got tax purposes as any option that you rollover does not need to be accounted for until it has been either purchased or expired. Play name: Straddle Who should run it: This strategy is suitable for everyone When to run it: This strategy is effective in a bullish or bearish market Details: The straddle can be used to either go long or short.

The long straddle can be extremely effective if you feel as though the price of a given underlying asset is going to move significantly in one direction, you don't know what direction that will ultimately be. To utilize this strategy, you will need to purchase a put and a call, both using the same underlying asset, strike price, and timeframe. After the long straddle has been created successfully, you will be guaranteed to generate a profit if the price in question moves in either direction before it expires. On the other hand, if you are interested in utilizing a short straddle, you will instead want to sell a call and a put with the same costs, timeframe, and underlying asset. This will allow you to profit from the premium, even if everything else doesn't turn out as well as you may have liked. This guaranteed Profit means that this is a particularly useful strategy if you don't expect to see movement very much in either direction before the option expires. Nevertheless, it is still important to remember that the chances that this strategy will be successful are directly related to the odds that the underlying asset is going to move in the first place. Play name: Strangle who should run it: This strategy is suitable for everyone When to run it: This strategy is effective in a bullish or bearish market Details: Functionally, a strangle similar to a straddle except that it is often cheaper to execute on as you are buying into options that are already out of the money. As such, you can typically pay as much as 50 percent the cost of a straddle for a strangle, which makes it even easier to play both sides of the fence.

Typically, a long strangle is more useful than a short straddle because it offers up twice the premium for the same amount of risk. To use the long strangle correctly, you will want to purchase a call along with a put that is both based on the same underlying asset with the same timeframe and different strike prices. The strike price for the call will need to be above the strike price for the put, and both should be out of the money. This strategy can be especially useful if you plan on the underlying asset moving a great deal, without having a clear idea as to the direction. When used properly, this will virtually ensure you turn a profit once you have taken any fees out of the equation. Play name: Butterfly spread who should run it: This strategy is suitable for everyone When to run it:

This strategy is effective in a neutral market Details: A butterfly spread is a combination of a bear spread and a traditional bull strategy which uses a total of three strike points. To begin with, you will need to purchase a call option at the lowest point you can manage before selling a pair of calls at a higher price and then a third call that has an ever-higher price. Your end goal with these purchases is to make sure that you have a range of prices you can profit from when everything is said and done. This strategy can prove particularly effective when you have a completely neutral opinion on the current market. What's more, you should also expect the underlying asset to move in the direction you favor, even if you don't have all the details locked down just yet. This, then means that you will want to strive to keep the market volatility as low as possible. The greater the overall level of volatility, the greater the cost of this strategy will be. Furthermore, it is imperative to keep in mind that if you choose incorrectly when it comes to the direction the underlying asset is going to move, then the amount you stand to lose can be significant. Play name: Iron condor Who should run it: This strategy is suitable for everyone When to run it: This strategy is effective in a bullish or bearish market Details: To utilize the iron condor strategy, you will need to begin by taking a short position as well as a long position via a pair of strangles that is situated so they will take full advantage of a market that is staunchly low volatility. The pair of strangles should include both a long and a short, with both sets to the outer strike price. You can accomplish the same general effect with a pair of credit spreads if you are so inclined. In this scenario, the call spread would be placed above the market price, and the put would be placed beneath the current market price. The iron condor should only be used if you are trading via index options as they offer the decreased level of volatility and risk that you need to make it reliable. This means that you will want to use the iron condor if you are practically certain the market is going to move in the direction your research indicates that it is going to. Doing otherwise is almost surely going to leave your plan open to significant additional risk, and likely sooner rather than later as well. Play name: Iron Butterfly Who should run it: This strategy is suitable for everyone When to run it: This strategy is effective in a bullish or bearish market Details: The iron butterfly strategy can be anchored by either a short straddle or a long straddle depending on your needs. Regardless, you will want to orchestrate than a strangle based on the straddle you needed to use. The iron butterfly utilizes a mixture of puts and calls to limit the potential for loss (but also profits) around the strike price you previously determined. This strategy is best used with options that are out of the money as they allow you to minimize both risk and cost.

When it comes to trading options successfully in the long-term, the secret isn't being able to make the right trades at every juncture. After all, that's impossible. No, the real secret to long-term success is learning to recover when a surefire trade suddenly goes sideways on you at the last moment. The faster you can get your business back on track, the quicker you can get back to making a profit. Long call repair strategies

Long call repair strategies

This first section contains strategies designed to increase the profit potential of long call positions that have recently seen a quick, unrealized loss. Remember, having a great strategy is extremely important, but there is more to making a profit in the long-term than that. In trading, the best offense is often a good defense. Play name: Long call repair Who should run it: This strategy is suitable for veterans When to run it: This strategy is effective in a bullish market Details: It is common for new traders to buy a simple put or call, only to find out that they were ultimately wrong about the way the underlying asset moved when everything was said and done. For example, a long call that is out of the money would see sudden unrealized losses if its underlying asset dropped. To understand the best course of action in this situation, a second example is required. For this example, assume that it is the middle of the February and you believe that Microsoft which is currently sitting at 93.30 is about to make a move that puts it above its resistance levels and end at about 95. You can then easily jump in with a near the money call for July, leaving you roughly six months until expiration and plenty of time for the related movement to occur. From there, however, things don't go according to plan, and the stock drops to below $90 instead. The price of your July call would now be worth only about $1.25, down from about $3 thanks to the time decay, creating an unrealized loss of $175 per option purchased.

As there is still a fair amount of time left until expiration, it is possible that the stock could still make the option profitable but waiting also has the potential to generate additional losses or other opportunity costs which could also result in a loss of Profit. One way to mitigate this loss is through the process of averaging down and purchasing additional options, though this only increases your risk if things continue not to go your way. Instead, a simple and effective means of lowering your breakeven point, while also increasing the possibility of turning a profit is to roll the position down into a bull call spread, discussed in the next chapter. The concept of rolling it down means to replace an existing option with a new option that is similar in most ways except that one has a lower strike price than the other. Utilizing this practice mans you don't have to exercise the first option as the time is extended until the end of the second option. To use this strategy in the above example, you would start by placing an order to sell a pair of calls at the July expiration date at your target price of $95 for $1.25, which is essentially going short on the first call option. At the same time, you would want to buy an additional July 90 call and sell it for roughly $2.90. The result of this process is a bull call spread that improves the odds of success while only adding a small amount of additional risk. What' more, the breakeven point decreases dramatically from $98, all the way to $93.25. From there, assuming that the Microsoft stock continued to trade even higher, past the original starting point, then your bull call spread would be strong enough to break even with a potential profit for the target of $95, though the maximum amount of Profit for each option is going to be $175 due to the way it was constructed. Play name: Alternate repair style Who should run it: This strategy is suitable for veterans When to run it: This strategy is effective in a bullish market Details: Alternately, you could roll down into a traditional butterfly spread, discussed in the next chapter when the underlying stock drops to $90. When using this strategy, you would instead want to sell a pair of July $90 calls, which would sell for about $4 each, while also hanging on to the July $95 long call. You would also need to purchase a call for the July date at $85 as well that sells for around $7.30 after time decay has been taken into account.

You will see that the total risk actually decreases on the downside in this scenario as the total debit amount drops to $230, and there is also a limited upside risk if the stock moves back towards the breakeven point. If the stock goes nowhere, the trade still turns a profit as well. Play name: Combined repair strategy Who should run it: This strategy is suitable for all-starts When to run it: This strategy is effective in a bullish market Details: As this is a variation of the traditional butterfly spread, the maximum amount of profit you can expect is going to come at the strike price of the two July $90 short calls that you created, but movement dropping away from this point until it starts to generate losses instead. As such, you may also want to combine the two repair strategies to create a multi-lot repair approach. This combination can be used to preserve the ideal odds that come with producing a profit from a potential loss. Determining strike price: One of the most important facets of using the repair strategy effectively is setting the correct strike price for the options in question. This price will ultimately determine the cost of the trade as well as influencing your breakeven point. The best place to start is by considering the magnitude of the unrealized loss that you are coming off of. For example, if you purchased a stock at $40 and it is now at $30, then your paper loss is $10 per share.

In this case, you would want to purchase the at the money calls while at the same time writing out of the money calls with a higher strike price that is above the strike price of the purchased calls by half of the stock's loss. This means you would want to start with three-month options before moving forward from there as needed. Generally speaking, the greater the loss you have already experienced, the greater the amount of time that you will have to spend repairing it. It is also important to keep in mind that it will not be possible to repair all mistakes for free as the worst offenders will require a small debit payment to set up the position in a potentially profitable manner. If your loss is over 70 percent, then it is likely not going to be possible to repair it at all.

Unwind the position: While breaking even after the hypothetical situations discussed above might sound good now, when you find yourself in a similar situation in the real world you may find yourself wanting to more than break even, you will likely want to make an additional profit as well. As an example, assume that the Microsoft stock that previously dropped now rose to $60, which means that you are now interested in keeping it rather than selling when it hits $70. Unwinding a position consists of closing out a positive that has previously been pulling double duty offsetting other investments. Unwinding can increase liquidity risk in some scenarios. If an asset is less liquid, it can be difficult to find an interested buyer or seller, which means the liquidity risk is elevated. Regardless of whether a transaction was completed intentionally or accidentally, all risks associated with the particular security still apply when attempting to unwind it. Unwinding becomes an even more advantageous proposition if the volatility in the underlying stock has increased to such a point that you decide you want to hold onto the stock. You will be able to find your options priced much more attractively in this scenario as long as you remain in a good position with the underlying stock. Problems can arise in this scenario if you attempt exiting while the stock is trading at or above the breakeven price as this will cost you as the total value of the option in question will be negative. As such, you should generally only consider unwinding an existing position if the price remains underneath the original breakeven price and the prospects look promising.

Otherwise, you are typically going to be better off simply establishing a new position in the same stock at the current market price. Short call repair strategies Play name: Delta hedge Who should run it: This strategy is suitable for veterans When to run it: This strategy is effective in a bullish or bearish market Details: To understand this strategy, consider the following. Let's say you own an exchange-traded call option on a listed stock (very general case). If available in sufficient quantity, borrow and sell the underlying security that the call option was written on (short sell it). You'll belong the call and short the stock. This is called a delta hedge, as you would be delta trading the stock. Delta refers to short-term price volatility. In other words, you'll short a single large block of the stock, then buy shares, in small increments, whenever the market drops slightly, on an intra-day basis. When the market price of the stock rises incrementally, you'll sell a few shares. Back and forth, in response to short-term market price moves, while maintaining a static "hedge ratio."

As your first call option gets closer to maturity, roll it over into the next available contract, either one-month or preferably three-month, time to expiration. Play name: Synthetic Short Who should run it: This strategy is suitable for veterans When to run it: This strategy is effective in a bearish market Details: The synthetic short is used to promote the payoff of a short losing position. It can be completed by selling a call that is currently at the money while at the same time buying an equal number of puts that are also at the money for the same underlying stock and expiration date. It is important to keep in mind that there are immense risks when it comes to using this strategy, along with an unlimited potential for Profit which means it is best used when you are bearish on the related underlying security.

You can think of this strategy as being similar to the short stock position as a whole as there is no maximum for Profit as long as the underlying stock price continues to drop. Furthermore, credit is typically taken when entering this scenario, as calls are almost always going to be more expensive than puts. This means that even if the underlying stock price remains relatively unchanged for the length of the expiration time, there will still be a potential for Profit based on the amount of the initial credit that was taken. The formula for determining a profit in this scenario is as follows: Maximum Profit = Unlimited Profit Achieved When Price of Underlying < Strike Price of Long Put + Net Premium Received Profit = Strike Price of Long Put - Price of Underlying + Net Premium Received As with the unlimited potential for reward, the potential for risk in this scenario, to determine the potential for loss, consider the following: Maximum Loss = Unlimited Loss

Occurs When Price of Underlying > Strike Price of Short Call + Net Premium Received Loss = Price of Underlying - Strike Price of Short Call-Net Premium Received + Commissions Paid Finally, the breakeven point in this scenario can be determined via the following: Breakeven Point = Strike Price of Long Put + Net Premium Received

Chapter 8: An Example of Trade

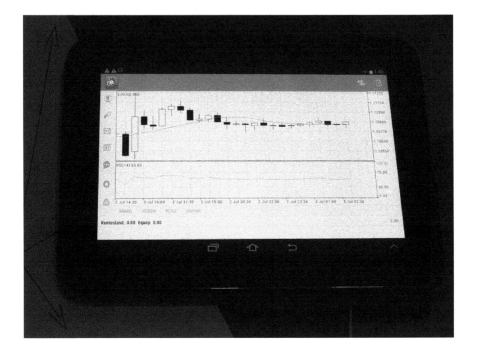

In this chapter, we will talk about basic trading habits, and also give you examples of some great option trading strategies. That way you have a better idea on how to go about trading. Keep in mind, this information can be used for any trading you decide to take part in. Keeping that in mind, we will dive into this chapter.

The investment in the medium and long-term is ideal for those who want to build capital, or simply diversify and enhance savings over time simply and at reduced costs. Given their versatility, ETFs can be used in different medium and long-term investment strategies, where they can support or replace traditional instruments, thus allowing to achieve the set objective. Currently, the range of ETFs is so diverse that any FCI can be replicated (at a much higher cost)

A strategy to invest its capital in the medium to long term is to resort to investment funds, whose popularity has grown progressively over the last twenty years. One of the main characteristics of the Funds is that of allowing the underwriter to enter the market with modest capital and to obtain professional management that will allow them to obtain positive results over time, with moderate risk. Investment funds should favor more active management, even if this does not always happen. In addition to weighing on their final return, they are the highest management costs to which the same funds are subject, and whose impact is felt particularly in times of slowdown or stagnation of the market. In light of this situation, the investor could find it convenient to substitute the investment in funds with that of ETFs that aim to follow closely the evolution of its benchmark index, while offering the maximum possible transparency.

In advance it cannot be said whether it is better to invest in funds or in ETF; to make this choice you have to decide if you want the manager to move away from the benchmark (and from which benchmark): this possibility is called "active risk." Active risk is not necessarily bad, because there are some managers who are actually better than others, but in reality, they are few and, not always, you can find them. If you decide to move away from the basic risk, you must be convinced that:

good managers exist;

that they can do better than their benchmark;

above all, be able to find them!

If you think you can complete each of the three phases, it is appropriate to rely on active funds, otherwise, ETFs are preferred because they cost less and carry precisely where you decided to go, without additional surprises.

The techniques for choosing the ETF that best suits your investment strategies are different; an interesting methodology is applied to sector rotation: the market as a whole is made up of different equity sectors, corresponding to the different economic sectors and their continuous alternation from the origin to the expansion and contraction phases. For this reason, the moments in which all the economic sectors grow or decrease simultaneously are quite rare. The concept of sector rotation is useful to identify, on the one hand, the stage of maturity of the current primary trend and on the other to select those sectors that have a growing relative strength. For example, sectors sensitive to changes in interest rates tend to anticipate both the minimums and the maximums of the market, while the sectors sensitive to the demand for capital goods or raw materials generally tend to follow the overall trend of the market with delay. Through ETFs, it is possible to take an immediate position on a specific stock, without necessarily being forced to buy the different securities belonging to that particular basket. In this way, it will be possible to obtain immediate exposure to this sector, benefiting at the same time as its growth in value, besides the advantages linked to the diversification.

It is also possible to invest using relative strength, investing, perhaps, on a stock exchange index, at the same time benefiting from its growth in value, in addition to the advantages linked to diversification.

For example, if one thinks that at a given moment the US market should grow in relative terms to a greater extent than the French one, it will be appropriate to make the first one and to underweight the second one. This decision can be reached by analyzing the comparative relative strength between the two markets, which compares two dimensions (composed of market, sector, securities or other indices) to show how these values are performing in a relative manner. Respect to each other. The trend changes expressed by relative strength generally tend to anticipate the actual ones of the financial activity to which it refers. It is, therefore, possible to use the relative strength to direct purchases towards ETFs that show a growing relative force.

The great flexibility of ETFs also allows the construction of guaranteed capital investment; in times of financial turbulence, investors often turn to products that provide capital protection: those provided by financial intermediaries often have high fees and charges for customers. Not many people know that it is possible to build a guaranteed capital product by yourself, which respects your personal investment needs! The central point of the logic of guaranteed capital is interest rates and the duration of the investment because at the base of all there are the two central concepts of finance:

the higher the interest rates, the greater the return on the money

as the duration increases, you earn more, because money "works" longer

The money we will obtain in many years can be brought to today, as for bills that follow the discount law (the technical term of bringing the future money to today). You can easily answer the question: "to have 100 euros in seven years, knowing that the rates are at 5%, how much money do I have to invest?" This statement indicates how much money is needed to invest today to get the desired amount at maturity. The bonds that allow only the fruits to maturity, without paying interest during their life, are called zero-coupon bonds (zcb) and are quite common on the market. If for example, I want to have € 100 at maturity and interest rates are at 5% I will have to invest in zero-coupon bonds € 95.24 (if the deadline is between 1 year) € 78.35 (if the deadline is in 5 years) € 61.39 (if the deadline is 10 years) 48.1 € (if the deadline is between 15 years) and 23.21 € (if the deadline is 30 years)

In effect, by building investment with guaranteed capital, one only has to decide how to invest the remaining part of the initial 100 euros that have not been allocated in the zero coupons. An ideal solution could be to invest in options because, thanks to the leverage effect, they can amplify any yield. If you have a less aggressive investment profile, ETFs are excellent tools to build guaranteed capital investment. If, for example, we assume a 10-year investment with rates of 2.5% for that maturity, the portion to be invested in zcb is equal to 78.12%, while the remaining 21.88% will be invested in ETF.

This investment strategy makes it possible to achieve a minimum (not real) "money" return target with few operations, as the zcb provides for the repayment only on the nominal amount of the loan (not discounted to the inflation rate). It is, therefore, a valid methodology for those who intend to make investments with clear objectives and have little time to devote to monitoring the values as only an operation until expiry may be necessary. Unlike a guaranteed capital product offered by any financial intermediary, an investment of this kind built independently with ETFs can be dismantled entirely or in pieces (selling only the zcb or active assets, ETF) to meet any need. Naturally, only at maturity will there be a certainty of the pre-established return and, over the course of the loan, a temporary adverse trend in financial variables, (rates rise by lowering the zcb and at the same time decreasing the value of the ETF) could result in the liquidation of losing positions. The same consequence would be selling a structured bond, with the advantage that "doing it at home" the commissions are much lower and you can separate the two components and, if necessary, liquidate only one, according to specific needs.

Profitability of equity (Roe): this is the ratio between the net result and the net assets of a given company, in particular from the point of view of equity investments is an important parameter as a profitability higher than the cost of capital is an index of the ability of an enterprise to create value, therefore it should be a guarantee of greater capacity for growth of the securities in the phases of the rise of the market and of resistance in the reflexive phases. From this point of view, the Roe is always held in strong consideration by those who choose to invest in shares today.

Price/earnings ratio: a low ratio of this parameter makes a share price particularly attractive, but at the same time it could mean that expectations regarding future profits are not particularly positive. As in the case of the Roe, this is a factor to be taken into due consideration when choosing the best actions to invest in.

Price-book value ratio: the ratio between the share price and the net asset value resulting from the last balance sheet, especially if this ratio is lower than the unit means that the company is being paid less than the value of the budget net of liabilities. However, this does not necessarily mean that it is a good deal, since the company may not be able to produce profits either.

Dividend yield: this is the percentage ratio between the last distributed dividend and the share price, in particular, it measures the remuneration provided by the company to shareholders in the last year in the form of liquidity. This parameter is often taken into account to identify the securities to invest in, since a company able to distribute dividends is generally a healthy company, but also in this case, as with all the other selection parameters, it is necessary to a broader and more complete analysis, since a high level of this indicator could also mean that the company has made few investments or has little prospect of growth. For this reason, looking at the dividend yield as a primary factor in determining the securities in which to invest in the options market is reductive. The dividend yield only makes sense if accompanied by considerations on any business plans and industrial plans of the listed company. Only in this way is it possible to have guarantees on what are the prospects of the group in the future.

Rating and target price: the rating is the judgment that certain analysts and investment banks have on a specifically listed security while the target price represents the maximum target price to which the security may go. Dozens of judgments are published daily on all listed shares. Giving an eye to these judgments is a way to have further clarification on what may be the prospects of the listed. If, in fact, more brokers decide to cut the rating on an X stock from buying (buy) to neutral or worse still sell (sell) then it means that, indeed, the expectations of the security in question are certainly not positive and therefore, perhaps, it is not the case to insert this title in the list of shares to invest in. Clearly, promotions and failures (upgrades and downgrades) are not in the air but are accompanied by reports within which are explained the reasons behind that single judgment. Therefore, rating and target price are one of the most important factors for choosing the best actions to invest in. More. As the great traders who focus on equities perfectly know, looking at the historian or the evolution of the rating and target price of a single stock, one can have an even more complete picture in the choice of actions to invest in today.

I have drawn the basic coordinates for the choice of securities to invest in. This brief guide does not clearly claim to be exhaustive but taking the factors indicated into consideration means reducing the risk margin in the investment. These considerations also apply clearly when investing in online shares through trading platforms. Before identifying the best stock to bet on, in fact, it is always good to take into account the parameters that we have indicated even if, as happens in the case of online trading, the goal is not to hold possession of the action but rather to bet on the price of the same.

As you can see in this chapter we talked about many things that will help you with the trading, more specifically option Trading. You have to understand that when it comes to option Trading it is very similar to stock trading and options trading. Keeping that in mind we gave you tips and examples on how trading the truly work. Moreover, we also showed you some of the tips that many top Traders use in order to make more money from the traits. This book is essentially a basic overview of options trading and trading in general. Also, once you understood this book you will be in a much better position to try and get for trading for yourself and expanding more. Also if there's anything in this book which you don't understand, make sure that you keep reading it until you do as it is very important that you do so. Understanding options trading or trading, in general, is a very difficult task, so we totally understand if you have to go through his book again to really understand the concept. With that in mind we come to the conclusion of this chapter, thank you so much for reading until the end and we hope you really learned a lot from this chapter.

Chapter 9: Tips for Becoming a Top Trader

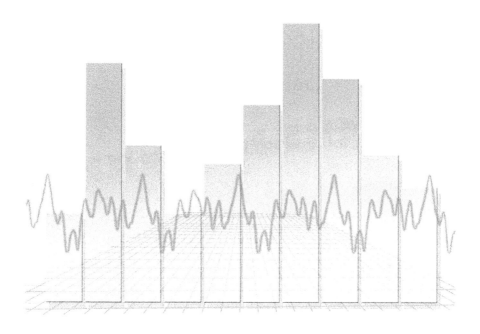

Successful Trading Strategies

When all is said in done, you are the one responsible for turning your venture into foreign exchange into a successful endeavor. That is actually one of the great things about the stock. You do not have a boss screaming down your neck, telling you to do something that you do not agree with. You have the ability to come up with your own trading plan based on your own research and your own knowledge. That being said, success can come more quickly for some than for others, and a lot of the time this has to do with approaching this endeavor with the right strategy. In this chapter, we will provide you with three strategies designed to help you make this foray into stock as profitable as possible (with as little loss as possible).

Strategy 1. Buy low and sell high.

This is a strategy that we have discussed before and it's not as straightforward as it seems. If you began stock trading today with $25,000 in your pocket and access to a trading platform, all ready and raring to go, how would you know what is low and what is high? It's your first day. Naturally, for you to understand what would represent a good low investment and conversely what is high, you need to have some knowledge of the exchange rate history of that currency. Maybe the exchange rate for Japanese yen seems low, but actually, compared to last year or a few months ago, it's a little high. Now it would not be a good time to buy. Maybe the pound seems low right now, but yesterday the British government announced that the first round of the Brexit negotiations with the EU failed and therefore the pound may have room to go lower than it is was when you logged onto your trading platform. Maybe you should wait and see what the pound is later today or tomorrow and buy then. The point here is that buying low and selling high requires understanding the patterns associated with that stock and what might cause it to go up or down. And that's merely the buying side of things. Once you have bought low, you need to figure out when you are going to sell. This is where a good trading plan will come into play. A good plan will prevent you from selling too soon, or even not selling soon enough.

Strategy 2. Focus on not losing money rather than on making money.

This may not be an easy strategy to understand initially, in part because not losing money and making money seem like two sides of the same coin. They are, but they are not identical. One of the personality types that is associated with difficulty in finding success in trading is the impulsive type. This type of person wants to make money and they want to make it quick. They have a vague strategy about how they plan on doing that, but the most important thing to them is that they have a high account balance to make as many trades as they need to turn a profit. This is the wrong approach. Currencies are not the same as stocks. The value of a stock may change very little even over a week's time, so I strategy that involves a lot of trades in order to make money is usually not the best strategy. You want to have a crystal clear idea of when you are going to but, yes, because you want to make money, but mostly because you don't want to lose.

Every market that involves exchanges, like the stock market, has some implicit risk, and stock trading is risky, too, because you may be tempted to give up the advantage you have to try and make money quickly.

Strategy 3. Develop a Sense of Sentiment Analysis

Alright, the third strategy was going to be about Fibonacci retracement, which is a type of technical analysis of the market, but as this is the basics of stock trading, we are going to go into a different strategy that is not any easier than a Fibonacci retracement, just different. Sentiment analysis is a term that is used in many different specialties, not just finance, and it is not easy to describe. It is essentially a type of analysis that is not based on a chart showing exchange rates over time (technical analysis) or on an understanding of a factor that might today be affecting the value of the stock(fundamental analysis). Sentiment analysis attempts to gauge the tone of the market, the direction the market is heading in, by parsing all of the available information. A key to understanding sentiment analysis is likening it to public opinion. The economy may be booming, people have more money in their pocket, so the stock of this hypothetical country should increase in value, but maybe it doesn't. Maybe there is something that is causing the market to be bearish and which therefore might cause the stock to drop. As you perhaps can tell, as this analysis is not based on any concrete information, it can be thought of as intuitive and no one has intuition on day 1. Let's just be honest about that. Intuition comes from experience. But the purpose of this strategy is to introduce to you the idea that not the foreign exchange market, like any market is not going to behave like a machine because it's not a machine. Markets are places where human beings come together and humans are unpredictable, often in a frustrating way. Perhaps one day, stock trading may be handled by machines (that wouldn't be fun), but that day is far off and so you will have to develop your own sense of where the market seems to be going and use this as a strategy to achieve success in this endeavor.

Research

Regardless of the investment that you make, be sure always to do your research. Doing research is a must. It is what will increase your chances of making the right investment decision. As the saying goes, "Knowledge is power." The more that you understand something, the more likely that you will be able to predict how it will move in the market. This is why doing research is essential. It will allow you to know if something is worth investing in or not. Remember that you are dealing with a continuously moving market, so it is only right that you keep yourself updated with the latest developments and changes, and the way to do this is by doing research.

Just because you have surfed the web for a few hours does not mean that you are already in the position to make an investment decision. You should understand that doing research should be part of your daily life as an investor/trader. Even if you are just a side trader, it is still essential that you do your research so that you will be informed of the best trading practices.

Remember that gaining information is not limited to just surfing the web for information. It is also suggested that you join online groups and forums that are related to your chosen investment. This way, you will be able to meet and connect with like-minded people. There is also a good chance that you can learn something from them.

Do not rush the process of doing research. Take note that you make decisions based on the information that you have on hand, and such information that you have will depend on the time and efforts that you put into doing research. Make sure that all of your decisions are backed up by solid research and analysis.

Write a Journal

Although not a requirement, writing a journal can be beneficial. You do not need to be a professional writer to write a memoir; however, you need to do two things: Update your journal regularly and be completely honest with everything that you write in your journal. By having a journal, you will be able to identify your strengths and weaknesses more effectively. It can also help you realize lessons that you might otherwise overlook.

You can record anything in your journal that is related to your business or investment. Ideally, it should contain your reasons, as well as your objectives. You can also write down your mistakes and new learning's that you encounter along the way.

In the first few weeks, you might not appreciate the value of keeping a journal. However, after some time, you will start to understand its importance, especially once you begin to notice your progress or developments. The important thing is to persist in writing your journal. It will allow you to view yourself from a new perspective, from a standpoint that is free from bias and prejudice.

Have a Plan

Whether you are going to start forex trading or trade in general, it is always good to have a plan. Make sure to set a clear direction for yourself. This is also an excellent way to avoid being controlled by your emotions or becoming greedy. You should have a short-term plan and a long-term plan. You should also be ready for any form of contingency. Of course, it is impossible to be prepared for everything. If you are suddenly faced with an unexpected and challenging situation, take your time to study the situation and develop a new plan. Never take action without proper planning. Poor planning leads to poor execution but having a good idea usually ends up favorably. You should stick to your plan. However, there are certain instances when you may have to abandon your project, such as when you realize that sticking to the same program will not lead to a desirable outcome or in case you find a much better idea. Proper planning can give you a sense of direction and ensure the success of execution.

Make your plans practical and reasonable. Remember that you ought to stick to whatever project you come up with, so be sure to keep your ideas real. Before you come up with an idea, you must first have quality information. Again, this is why doing research is very important.

What if you fail to execute your plan? This is not uncommon. If this happens to you, relax and think about what made you fail to stick to your plan? Was it favorable to you or not? Take some time to analyze the situation and learn as much as you can from it. Indeed, having a plan is different from executing it. It is more challenging to implement a plan as it demands that you take positive actions.

Learn from Your Competitors

Pay attention to your competitors and learn from them. Studying your competitors is also an excellent way to identify your strengths and weaknesses. You can learn a great deal from your competitors, especially ideas on how you can better improve your business.

Your competitors can also help you promote your trading goals and draw more techniques. This way, you get a better idea of how to trade. You do not have to fight against your competitors; you can work together.

It is prevalent for people online to support one another. , it is a good practice that you connect with other traders, especially those who are in the same niche. Do not think of them as your direct competitors, and you might be surprised just how friendly they can be.

Now, a common mistake is to consider yourself always better than the others. This is wrong as you are only deluding yourself, making you fail to see the bigger picture. Instead of still seeing yourself better than your competitors, learn from them, and see how you can use this knowledge to improve your trading endeavors

Cash-out

Some people who trade forex or invest in cryptocurrency commit the mistake of not making a withdrawal. The reason why they do not cash out is so that they can grow their funds. Since you can only earn a percentage of what you are trading/investing, having more funds in your account means that you can make a higher profit return. Although this may seem reasonable, it is not a recommended approach. It is strongly advised that you should request a withdrawal. You should understand that the only way to truly enjoy your profits is by turning them into cash; otherwise, it is only as if you were using a demo account. Also, by making a withdrawal, you get to lower your risks, since the funds that you withdraw will no longer be exposed to risks. You do not have to remove all your profits right away. If you want, you can withdraw 30% of your total profits, allowing the remaining 70% to add up to the funds in your account. The important thing is to make a withdrawal still now and then.

Take a Break and Have Fun

Making money online can be fun and exciting; however, it can also be a tiring journey. Therefore, give yourself a chance to take a break from time to time. When you take a break, do not spend that time thinking about your online business. Instead, you should spend it to relax your body and clear your mind. If you do this, then you will be more able to function more effectively. This is an excellent time to go on a vacation with your family or friends or at least enjoy a movie night at home. Do something fun that will put your mind off of business for a while. Do not worry; after this short break, and you are expected to work even more.

Making money online is a long journey, so enjoy it. Making money online can be lots of fun. Do not just connect with people to build a good following, but also try to make friends with your connections. You do not have to take things too seriously. Keep it fun and exciting.

Conclusion

Thank you so much for purchasing the book options trading: Advanced Guide to Make Money Trading Options in 30 Days or Less! – Learn the Fundamentals and Profitable Strategies of Options Trading.

As you can see, we learn many things in this book. Not only did we teach you how to set up a profitable options trading portfolio, but we also showed you how to make a lot of money and take it to the next level with options trading. Options trading is one of the less risky ways to make money with trading, and nonetheless, if not done correctly, then you will pay the price. Options trading is